DEMOCRACY
— *in* —
HEAVEN

the cause of satan's exile

MARK McCAULEY

Copyright © 2019 by Mark McCauley.

ISBN   Softcover   978-1-949723-72-4

All rights reserved. No part of this book may be reproduced or transmitted in any form or by any means, electronic or mechanical, including photocopying, recording, or by any information storage and retrieval system without express written permission from the author, except in the case of brief quotations embodied in critical reviews and certain other non-commercial uses permitted by copyright law.

Printed in the United States of America.

To order additional copies of this book, contact:
Bookwhip
1-855-339-3589
https://www.bookwhip.com

This book is based on the 66 books of the Bible.

This is a true saying: "God chooses the foolish things of this world to confound the wise..." (1 Corinthians 1:27).

I'm grateful God chose me, a fool, to confound the wise.

This is also a true saying: "The foolishness of God is wiser than man's wisdom..." (1 Corinthians 1:25).

TABLE OF CONTENTS

Acknowledgements vii
Words of Wisdom ix
Introduction xi

War in Heaven 1
Plan and Purpose 6
    The Plan of God Before Creation of Heaven and Earth 6
    The Purpose 9
Before the Beginning 13
    Before Heaven and Earth, Where Was God? 13
    God Separated Eve From Adam and Reserved Her to
    be the Mother of All Living, or Humanity 15
The Greatness of God 18
    God Transcends His Creation 18
    Jesus Was Not Created; He Was Separated 19
God Enters His Creation 26
    God Stepped Into His Creation, First in Heaven as
    Angel of the Lord, Second on Earth as Son of God,
    or Son of Man 26
The Other Dimension 29
    Is God a Person, Place, and Thing? 29
Before the Fall 32
Kings and Kingdoms 39
    Three Types of Kingdoms 39
    What Constitutes a King or Kingdom? 42
The Kingdom of God 50

The Kingdom of Satan 58
    The Counterfeit Kingdom 58
The Kingdom of Men 64
    Democracy, The Last Government 64
    Types of Governments 65
Before the Organization (Government) of Mankind 71
Exile: The Banishment of Satan 73
    The Tale of a Mad Angel 73
    God's Identity Has Been Compromised (Identity Theft) 76
    Exiled to Earth 84
Fugitives 89
    Satan and His Demons Escape Exile 89
    The Tale of a Mad Angel 95
    What Is The Forbidden Fruit? 102
Christian Nation What Constitutes a Christian Nation? 115
    Should Christians Go to War? 119
    Testament 121
    Christians Killing Christians 127
Mark of the Beast 133
    Unveiling the Mark Of The Beast 133
    The Second Curse 137
    The Mark of Circumcision 139
    God Marks His People Corporately 140
    The First Plague – Water to Blood 142
    The Second Plague – Frogs 143
    The Third Plague – Gnats or Lice 144
    The Fourth Plague – Flies 144
    The Fifth Plague Livestock Disease 145
    The Sixth Plague – Boils 146
    The Seventh Plague Thunder and Hail 147
    The Eighth Plague – Locusts 148

    The Ninth Plague – Darkness 150
    The Tenth Plague Death of the Firstborn 150
Armageddon 154
    God Knows Us By Name, The Devil By Number 154
    Armageddon (The Last War or the Omega War) 157
    The Purpose of the Man of Sin Being Revealed 161

ACKNOWLEDGEMENTS

I want to thank my Lord and Savior and Father, Jesus Christ, Creator of heaven and earth, for his goodness toward me that led to repentance. Father God, by the power of the Holy Spirit, I love you in the name of Jesus Christ. Thank you for salvation. Amen.

I want to thank my beautiful wife of Twenty-three years of marriage, Zolinka McCauley. No other woman can complete me like you do, and I love you as Christ loved the Church and gave his life for it. I want to thank my beautiful children, Nerissa, Amani, Mark Jr., and Christian McCauley for being a gift to me; your inspiration in my life is what prompts me to pray to God to make me a good father to you. I want to thank my father, Anthony McCauley; stepmom, Marie; my sisters, Alice, Hannah, and Esther; and my nieces and nephews, especially Jeter Jones and Antonio, Erica, and Shanai McCauley. I want to also thank my inlaws for their unconditional love and my friends for their support. I want to also thank Men of Faith Intercessory Integrity Prayer (BFIIP.com) for their continual prayer and holding each other accountable. I would like to thank every pastor, minister, elder, deacon, and evangelist for their faithfulness to our Lord and Savior Jesus Christ. I pray that your faith be strengthened. Most importantly, I want to thank the body of Christ for its continual prayer and supplication before the almighty God our Father and his beloved Son, Jesus Christ, for our faith, hope, love, and integrity as Christians. I want to thank the editors, graphic designers, publicists, marketers, etc., for their help in fine tuning this book.

WORDS OF WISDOM

King Solomon was the wisest man to live, yet he lacked one thing: integrity.

Wisdom without integrity lacks guidance.

-

Scripture teaches that a child left to himself will shame is parents; so will every Christian who does not walk in integrity. They shame their maker.

-

When children are not trained in the way of the Lord, when they are old, they will hate the ways of God.

-

Any lusts or desires uncontrolled will corrupt good character.

-

INTRODUCTION

First of all, let me be the first to say that I like democracy in comparison to all other earthly governments. However, I love the kingdom of God more in comparison to democracy and other all earthly governments. Democracy is neither good nor bad, just like any other earthly government. It is as bad or as good as the integrity of the leader. Scripture puts it this way: "When the righteous are in authority, the people rejoice: but when the wicked beareth rule, the people mourn" (Proverbs 29:2, KJV).

Therefore, democracy's value is based on the righteousness of the leader. Then again, it really depends on whom you ask. If you force democracy upon a nation, I don't care how integral you are, you strip the people of their right and freedom to choose. I know one thing; anything that is forced upon a people or taken to the extreme becomes an error. Therefore, democracy is only good when the people want that institution of government. Whatever is forced upon a people cannot be good, because you take away their power of choice. And when a people's choices are taken away, oppression rules them. Thus, the spread of democracy is good for some people, while for others, it is oppressive. However, when we look at the kingdom of democracy in comparison to the kingdom of God, we see that they oppose one another. The kingdom of men or democracy is contrary to the kingdom of God. For instance, the kingdom of God, which is an absolute monarchy, is contrary to the kingdom of men, which derives its power from the people. Which kingdom will ultimately prevail? As we parallel the two kingdoms and examine the weakness and strengths of the kingdom of men, we will see that only one victor will emerge to annihilate its opposition and to forever establish a kingdom with no weakness and no end. The victor will be the kingdom of God, since it is without weakness. As we examine the progression and advancement of the kingdom of men, we see evil forces lurking in the shadows, forcefully gaining favor with all the affairs of men and deceptively uniting them to oppose the kingdom of God.

The people have rejected truth, so their consciousness has been snared by an ancient evil that seeks to bring total destruction and damnation upon the human race. As hard as it may seem to comprehend, the human race is oblivious to this global destruction that stems from these ancient, evil spirits, whose main intention is revenge. These spirits bring vengeance upon God's creation and God's people in the human world because they have been cast out of heaven, and the only way they can seek revenge from God is to seek the destruction of anything created in his image—his children, particularly those who, by reason, have accepted Jesus Christ as Lord and Savior. These ancient, evil spirits are wise and intelligent; they have managed to usurp the dominion given to mankind and now rule mankind with a vengeance of destroying all that is called God. They have managed to deceive mankind into thinking that evil is good and good is evil through a process of tolerance or acceptance. They make laws that violate God but are comfortable for evil habitation with the human race. There are those who willingly or ignorantly promote and advance these ancient, evil-spirit agendas. And there are those who know the truth but are afraid to stand up for it. Truth is not readily received in this modern world; in fact, those who dare speak the truth are either killed, severely punished, or demonized through character assassination. However, when you love someone or your country, speaking the truth becomes the right you exercise at your expense in hopes of freeing those who are in bondage and are oblivious to the truth. Death becomes the price of love that one pays for all to be free. Jesus Christ's death on the cross epitomizes this truth; by his death, I am free; by his stripes, I am healed. When you love, you speak the truth, without worrying about the consequences or the pain that may result, because love is not selfish. The controlling principle is this: "truth shall make you free"; if this principle is true, then failure to tell the truth will keep people in bondage, which is the nature of a lie, and if the truth will make you free, then a lie will bring you to captivity or bondage. Brothers and sisters, please pray for me as I boldly reveal the truth concerning the progression of mankind and the deceptions perpetuated upon God's chosen people by the devil and his agents — both demons and humans who consciously or subconsciously promote the devil's agenda. This agenda is Satan's desire to be God, which led to the first war in heaven.

WAR IN HEAVEN

God was on the throne exuberating the worship of the angels as they cried out, "Holy, holy, holy is the Lord God Almighty." Lucifer, aka Satan, was the lead worshiper, leading all the host of angels, or God's Sons; in praise, worship, and adoration to the most supreme God. All of a sudden, there was a great commotion. Lucifer gave the word to one third of the angels who had vowed to help him establish his own kingdom in heaven to attack the throne of God. Michael, the chief commander of God's army, and his angels were already briefed by Jesus — the Word of God — as to the coming *coup d'état*.

> And there was war in heaven: Michael and his angels fought against the dragon; and the dragon fought and his angels, And prevailed not; neither was their place found any more in heaven." And the great dragon was cast out, that old serpent, called the Devil, and Satan, which deceiveth the whole world: he was cast out into the earth, and his angels were cast out with him.
>
> Revelation 12:7-9 (KJV)

Michael, the chief commander of God's army, and his angels were victorious; they defeated Satan and his angels. They bound Satan and his angels in chains and brought them before the throne of the Triune God (Father, Son, and Holy Spirit). Satan and his angels were expelled out of heaven, out of the presence of God, and were banished to earth to await their final fate. Jesus Christ (Son) told us that he witnessed Satan fall like lightening from heaven:

> And he said unto them, I beheld Satan as lightning fall from heaven.
>
> Luke 10:18 (KJV)

They were exiled to earth, eternally separated from the marvelous light of God, which illuminates and empowers every angel created. They were thrust in utter darkness, away from the presence of God, trapped between time and space; they could not influence earth, because they were immaterial beings. They occupied the air, that's why Scripture says Satan is the prince of the air.

> Wherein in time past ye walked according to the course of this world, according to the prince of the power of the air, the spirit that now worketh in the children of disobedience: Among whom also we all had our conversation in times past in the lusts of our flesh, fulfilling the desires of the flesh and of the mind; and were by nature the children of wrath, even as others.
>
> Ephesians 2:2-3 (KJV)

When they were exiled to earth, they witnessed the relationship Adam and Eve had with Father God, their creator. Father God would come during the cool of day and commune with Adam and his wife Eve. They envied that fellowship, especially Satan. Satan and his demons observed from behind the scenes and witnessed the moment God gave Adam dominion over all the earth, to rule and subdue over everything or anything that creeps, crawls, and flies within the earth's realm. How else would Satan know that God said to not eat from the tree of knowledge of good and evil when he was tempting Eve? He is not all knowing (Genesis 3:1, KJV). The devil and his demons were very upset when they witnessed God crown Adam, the king of all of earth and the creation of a queen, the king's companion and a suitable helpmate who would assist him with his dominion over earth.

So Satan and his corrupt wisdom sought to sever the fellowship and communion between God, Adam and his wife, with the hopes that Father God would banish them if they disobeyed his command. So Satan used the same trick he once used on one third of the angels that fell with him by deceiving Adam and Eve into disobeying God. This forced God to expel Adam and his wife from the garden of Eden just like the angels were expelled out of heaven for their treasons against Father God. This act of disobedience toward God, instigated by Satan, caused mankind to free Satan and his demons from exile and opened the door for Satan and his demons to enter the human world. The disobedience of Adam and Eve brought death upon the human world, as Satan and his demons sought revenge on all humans, created in the image of God. Satan and his demons escaped from exile and sought refuge and asylum within the human world by sharing or possessing the human body to materialize their revenge against God. With this new found shelter within the human race, they quickly began to infiltrate the affairs of mankind with their wisdom and sought to destroy all those who aimed to please God. As an example, Cain killed his righteous brother, Able, because Able's offering pleased God. The infiltration of these fallen angels upon mankind was so atrocious that God was grieved with mankind. God was sorry he had created mankind because the wickedness of mankind was great, so great in fact that God decided to destroy all of mankind. But before he did so, he had to find and preserve a man for the continuation of the human race. So Noah found favor with God and made a covenant with him to spare him and his family to regenerate him and to infiltrate them with his righteousness based on his own merits regardless of their sin and shortcomings until the promised seed was manifested to redeem mankind from the course of the law and the infiltration of these fallen angels. The goal of these fallen angels is to demonize the world by controlling and reshaping the thinking of mankind to contradict and counteract against God's laws, to hinder all relationship with God through ignorance of God's universal law and to formulate a world government that gives them supreme power over the human race and all human affairs. They long to create a demonic world that provides comfort to Satan and his demons to cohabitate with mankind while at the same time to finalize their ultimate plans of retaliation for being cast out of heaven and against the second coming of Jesus Christ.

This deadly deception has brought humanity to a brink of eternal extinction through a global deception perpetuated by Satan the adversary, the god of this world, and his demons and dehuman agents (humans that act like demons). Ever since the beginning, mankind, under the subtle influence of the devil has sought out government that will alienate God, the Creator of heaven and earth from his creation. Ever since his escape from exile into the human world, Satan has been influencing and recruiting mankind to join his army and is preparing them for the final war, the war of the world (Armageddon), where mankind, under the leadership of Satan and his demons join forces to fight against God the creator, Jesus Christ and his angels.

> And I saw three unclean spirits like frogs come out of the mouth of the dragon, and out of the mouth of the beast, and out of the mouth of the false prophet. For they are the spirits of devils, working miracles, which go forth unto the kings of the earth and of the whole world, to gather them to the battle of that great day of God Almighty.
>
> Revelation 16:13-14 (KJV)

This battle of Armageddon is the final, the omega, of all wars. The foolishness of men and their lust for power has finally brought them to the brink of extinction; their last hope, their final attempt to seek out their own world where man and Satan rule and live as one is hinged upon the victory of this war. But wisdom tells me that it is no contest; it's a lost cause, false hope and a fatal deception that will forever, eternally thrust Satan and his demons along with mankind (those who have rejected Jesus Christ as Lord and Savior) into the abyss of eternal damnation. The truth is Satan and his demons know that their cause is hopeless, yet they won't tell these earthly kings the truth because they are liars that continue to deceive mankind into believing they can be victorious over God. No matter how many nuclear weapons they make, no matter how many guns and war machines they test in preparation for the war of Armageddon, there is no hope. The only hope that remains is for the humans to repent from their sins by accepting Jesus Christ as Lord and Savior and renounce their allegiance to Satan and his demons. Yet Satan and his demons persist in leading mankind into a global decimation. They are combing through earth, recruiting mankind through subtle deceptions. For instance, they say that mankind will be invaded by aliens. They implore mankind to defend itself to preserve the hope of our children and our prosperity. In fact, the only alien we will see coming out of the sky is Jesus Christ at his second coming; as scripture says, every eye shall see him in the sky. This Hollywood, scripted invasion is designed to entertain and to condition our mind to think that the Creator of heaven and earth is an alien that plans to invade our civilization. And so we are told to prepare to fight to defend our right to exist without God.

PLAN AND PURPOSE

THE PLAN OF GOD BEFORE CREATION OF HEAVEN AND EARTH

To every plan there is a purpose; to every purpose there is a plan. My former pastor always echoes the following principle: "Failure to plan is plan for failure." It never dawned on me until I one day realized I was just living, with no sense of direction. I realized all the goals I had for myself were just dreams or wishful thinking because it did not come with a predetermined plan or strategy to make my goals a reality. All throughout my teenage years, especially before I started to live on my own, I was a failure because I never had a plan, so I lived a defeated lifestyle. I had no plan for my life or for my future. I lived life spontaneously, not worrying or thinking about tomorrow. As I continue to reflect back on my life, I realize that all throughout my life, it was God's plans for me that sustained me spiritually and my parents' obedience to God's plans for me that sustained me physically. It was my parents' plan for me that sustained a roof over my head, provided food for my stomach and clothes for me to wear, and chose the school I attended based on my grades or my neighborhood, etc.

> For even when we were with you, this we commanded you, that if any would not work, neither should he eat.
>
> 2 Thessalonians 3:10, (KJV)

I did not work; all of these were a result of my parents' vision for my life, particularly my father who raised me and my two sisters. God's influences over my father's life and his obedience to Him protected and shielded me physically and spiritually; it kept me from harm's way. As an illustration, we recall the story of Jesus Christ's birth and how King Herod sought to destroy him because the wise men came and asked him, "Where is he, who is born king of the Jews?" And through Joseph and Mary's obedience to God, Jesus' life was saved.

> And being warned of God in a dream that they should not return to Herod, they departed into their own country another way. And when they were departed, behold, the angel of the Lord appeareth to Joseph in a dream, saying, Arise, and take the young child and his mother, and flee into Egypt, and be thou there until I bring thee word: for Herod will seek the young child to destroy him. When he arose, he took the young child and his mother by night, and departed into Egypt: And was there until the death of Herod: that it might be fulfilled which was spoken of the Lord by the prophet, saying, Out of Egypt have I called my son. Then Herod, when he saw that he was mocked of the wise men, was exceeding worth, and sent forth, and slew all the children that were in Bethlehem, and in all the coasts thereof, from two years old and under, according to the time which he had diligently inquired of the wise men. Then was fulfilled that which was spoken by Jeremiah the prophet, saying, in Rama was there a voice heard, lamentation, and weeping, and great mourning, Rachel weeping for her children, and would not be comforted, because they are not.
>
> Matthew 2:12-18 (KJV)

Many times, if it was not for God's provision or plan for our life and our obedience to God, half of us would not be here today. Or, let me speak for myself; I would not be here today. Even though these plans did not guarantee an easy life or a stressfree life, through our parents' instructions, we were kept out of harm's way. The trouble I did get into due to my stubbornness did not kill me or put me in jail for the rest of my life but it was sufficient enough to cause great pain. And I learned great lessons from it. Because of this reality, the fifth commandment speaks loudly to me. When it says: "Honour thy father and thy mother: that thy days may be long upon the land which the Lord thy God giveth thee"(Exodus 20:12, KJV), I realize that all of life is planned, whether you planned it or it is planned for you, either by God, your parent, or by the enemy. Oh yes, the enemy has a plan for you, and his plan is to steal, kill, and destroy you (John 10:10, KJV). In fact, it was his plan that got him thrown out of the kingdom of heaven and caused one third of God's angels to lose their position in heaven and ultimately their relationship with God. Why would one third of God's sons or angels follow Satan's plan to overthrow God? Did he promise them something? What was this plan? What did he promise them? Could it be that he promised them a higher position in his government if successful? Was his plan to overthrow God by instituting a democratic government by which he would empower the angels to hold elections, to vote him into power, so he could be their god? What kind of government did God have since he was the king and had an army? For we know that anyone who has an army and is a king must run a government or a kingdom. The kingdom of God is a monarchy. Contrary to popular belief, the kingdom of God is not a theocracy because it is not a religious state in heaven. It is simply Father God and his sons (angels) living as a family. A theocratic kingdom exists only with respect to the kingdom of man who has established religious states and has chosen God to govern them. In the kingdom of God, God is the absolute ruler. He alone makes all decisions and whatsoever he speaks is law. He is the one who chooses who should be in his kingdom, not the angel. Lucifer wanted to change the order around in heaven by attempting to empower the angels to voice their opinion to challenge God's authority and to eventually vote him (Satan) into power as their new god. His plan failed miserably in heaven but managed to deceive and trick mankind into embracing it here on earth; as a result, mankind, and therefore all early governments not submitted to God are under the satanic influences. This is why the scripture says, "Satan is the god of this world" (2 Corinthians 4:4, KJV). And as we draw close to the end of the world, we see that Satan has introduced this plan to mankind, mankind has embraced this plan, and as a result, we see that in a democratic system, power is temporarily lodged in the hands of the people until the person is put in office. Then he exercises the power that is given to him by the people, for the people or against the people, based on the integrity of his heart. If he is not a man of integrity, he will renege on the promises he made to the people after he has been sworn in or taken his throne. Once the person is in office, he exercises all the power entrusted to him based on his own discretion regardless of what the people think or feel.

God knew all of this was in Lucifer, aka Satan's, heart before he even created the heavens and the earth. Because he is all knowing, he knew the rebellion that was going to take place in heaven. And as a result of the rebellion in heaven, he knew that Satan and his demons were going to entice mankind to join them in rebelling against God. Based on God's foreknowledge, he planned and set forth his plan in motion, before he even created us. This is why Scripture teaches that the "Lamb of God was slain before the foundation of the world" (Revelation 13:8, KJV); this why Scripture also teaches that God made man a "little lower than the angels" (Psalm 8:5, KJV); this is why Scripture also teaches that to whom he foreknew he predestined them to become the sons of God, (Roman 8:29, KJV), etc. All of this I will explain in the coming chapters.

THE PURPOSE

You can have a plan, but if you don't implement the plans, it is just a wish; however, the wish that you often have, if you act upon it according to plans, will soon become a reality. For example, any child that wishes to be a scientist, doctor, lawyer, basketball player, football player, etc., can make fulfill that wish by preparing and executing a plan and by taking the necessary steps to ensure that they receive good grades, stay in school, stay on track, and are focused on achieving those goals. A plan without implementation is wishful thinking. However, life without a plan is a plan that you live unknowingly; therefore, whoever strategizes your plan is the one who determines your end (Proverb 16:9, KJV).

God had planned for us way before he created the heavens and the earth and he strategized his plans through the implementation of covenants, whereby he could one day come and save us from our sins. He planned and calculated Satan's rebellion in heaven and his deception upon mankind and through the implementation of his plan, he brought us victory on Calvary; the cross where the Lamb of God was sacrificed. His plan for our lives is to preserve every one of us, to give us an expected future by giving us abundant life through Jesus Christ. Anyone who embraces his plan will live forever with him and not die. His plan was not only to preserve us but also to inform us of the gift he has placed in everyone of us and to accomplished the purpose for which he created us and also came and died for us. For example, I am reminded of the thoughts that God said he had for the prophet Jeremiah: "'For I know the thoughts that I think toward you,' saith the Lord, 'thoughts of peace, and not of evil, to give you an expected end'" (Jeremiah 29:11, KJV).

All of God's creation is planned. Creation is a brilliant and planned act from God. This is why scriptures say that the Lamb of God Jesus Christ) was slain before the foundation of the world. God thought everything through before he even made the heavens and the earth, which I will prove to you in the pages to come. Jesus's coming to die for our sins was planned a long, long time ago, way before the heavens and earth were created. He died on the cross for our sins and thereafter completed the implementation of that plan; that's why while on the cross, he uttered, "It is finished." What was finished? The atonement of our sins, based on his plans. This is also why creation is not by coincidence or a result of a big bang. The big bang theory contradicts the principle of design, which states, "In order for there to be a designed there have to be a purpose." Which simply means that whoever is responsible for the design had a reason in mind. No one designs or creates without a purpose—the essence behind the design or creation. Creation was designed by God; therefore, it has a purpose. If we accept the big bang theory, which simply states that creation came about through an explosion that resulted when energy and matter collided, then there is no intelligent design behind it which means all of creation is without purpose. There is no reason for creation or our existence because there is no intelligent design behind it. I refuse to believe in such deception that we as a human race evolved from animals. God created me for a reason, and we all have a purpose here on earth. Like the scriptures says, I am fearfully and wonderfully made (Psalm 139:14, KJV). The big bang theory does not make sense because there is nothing created that does not have a purpose for existing. Everything has a purpose and a designer behind it.

Our parents' plan for our lives is not based on democracy, where the children participate in the parent's decisions. Children are not asked to cast a vote, lot, or ballot to hold an election on where to live, what to eat, or the bills to pay, etc.; it is the parents who decide without the influence of their children. This is how God's kingdom is. As I look back and examine my life, I am very grateful for God's provision and his undying love for me. My parents' obedience to God brought about guidance and protections for my life. The decisions they made and the prayers they offered affected me both positively and negatively. And guess what? I was not part of the decision-making that indirectly shaped the course of my life. These decisions gave me a predetermined plan for my life because I was too young to know how to plan for my future. As I became mature, I am now able to plan my own life building on the foundation my parents laid for me. Now that I'm older and have my own kids, I am indirectly planning their future until they come of age; until they are old enough to plan their own future. Because underage children have no clue of what life is about, they do not have enough sense to carve out their own destiny. Therefore, I determine what school they go to, what they eat, where they should sleep, what bills are paid first, how they should dress, etc. This is the same way God treats us; we as children of God have no idea what eternal life is all about, nor do we have enough sense or knowledge to carve out our own eternity. All these decisions are not based on democracy; they are not negotiable, nor are they a result of my children grouping together to influence my decision. Nevertheless, since I'm not all knowing, and I'm a man and subject to error, my choices and decisions are motivated and rooted by my love for my children. Similarly, God is all knowing and his decisions are rooted based on his love for us. What I am simply saying is, I ultimately have the last word; I make decisions within my household based on what is best for the family. But my decision is based on me asking God for guidance, desiring to go where God wants me to go, do what God wants me to do. In that way, I know that God's favor and protection is upon me and my family. This is what I called living a planned life unknowingly. When it comes to our spiritual salvation or our birth into the world, it was all God's plan, because we had no choice in it; God did not consult us as to what family we would like to be born into or what neighborhood or country we should grow up in. We live in his plan unknowingly because we are not wise enough or mature enough to instruct God on how best we should be saved or what family or race we should be born to. Its God's plan of atonement, and he paid the price for all our sins so that we won't have to worry about working out a plan for salvation or how to atone for our salvation. It is a free gift; it is what we call a Father's love (John 3:16-17, KJV).

BEFORE THE BEGINNING

BEFORE HEAVEN AND EARTH, WHERE WAS GOD?

There lives an infinite being that is before creations, that is self-existing. He has no mother, no father, no genealogy, no beginning of days or ending of life. This being is called God, He alone is God, and there is no one like him. He alone is omniscient (all knowing), He alone is omnipotent (all powerful), he alone is omnipresent (he's everywhere), He alone is immutable (he's unchangeable), and He alone is eternal (he lives forever). Before creation, he was, and after creation, he is and will always be, even when the garments of heaven and earth get old or when they roll up like a scroll, he will be. He fathered all of creation; he's the giver and taker of life. Before him, there was no God formed, neither shall there be any God after him, for he was and still is before the beginning, even before time began. He existed alone and is complete in himself. All things exist in him and through him; without him, there is nothing that will exist. He is complete in himself; he's one but many (Elohim), a multiplicity of himself, meaning he is $1 \times 1 \times 1 \times 1 \times 1 \times 1 ... x1 = 1$(the Godhead), a multitude of persons yet A-L-O-N-E, meaning all one, all in one, or one in all. Just as when he created Adam as one yet many, like himself; in the image of God, he created him male and female. He made Adam one, yet more than one, a multitude of persons, complete and *alone*, all one or all in one. He made Adam and gave them (Adam) dominion over everything he created and told them (Adam) to be fruitful and multiply. He gave dominion to Adam over the fish of the sea, the fowl of the air, and over everything that creeps or crawls. It was only Adam that God gave the dominion to because God commanded only Adam not to eat from the forbidden fruits (Genesis 2:16-17, KJV), and Adam instructed Eve of God's command that he not eat the forbidden fruits.

> God said, Let us make man in our image, after our likeness: and let them have dominion over the fish of the sea, and over the fowl of the air, and over the cattle, and over all the earth, and over every creeping thing that creepeth upon the earth. So God created man in his own image, *in the image of God created he him; male and female created he them.*
>
> Genesis 1:26-27 (KJV) [emphasis mine]

This states "God created he him; male and female, created he them." This was only referring to Adam, not Eve, for Adam was considered both male and female, not by sexual orientation or sex but by gender, being created in the image and likeness of God, thus making him a son of God, man as angel or a little lower than the angel. For angels do not have sex, nor are they given into marriage, says Jesus Christ.

> The same day came to him the Sadducees, which say that there is no resurrection, and asked him, Saying, Master, Moses said, If a man die, having no children, his brother shall marry his wife, and raise up seed unto his brother. Now there were with us seven brethren: and the first, when he had married a wife, deceased, and, having no issue, left his wife unto his brother: Likewise the second also, and the third, unto the seventh. And last of all the woman died also. Therefore in the resurrection whose wife shall she be of the seven? for they all had her. Jesus answered and said unto them, Ye do err, not knowing the scriptures, nor the power of God. For in the resurrection they neither marry, nor are given in marriage, but are as the angels of God in heaven.
>
> Matthew 22:23-30 (KJV)

But as man or little lower than the angels are they categorically sexed and therefore they can be given into marriage, for procreation.

> What is man, that thou art mindful of him? And the son of man, that thou visitest him? For thou hast made him a little lower than the angels, and hast crowned him with glory and honour. Thou madest him to have dominion over the works of thy hands; thou hast put all things under his feet.
>
> Psalm 8:4-6 (KJV)

Note that scripture is twofold because it references mankind through the descendant of Adam and Eve, but its prophecy refers to Jesus Christ (see also Hebrews 2:7-9 (KJV).

GOD SEPARATED EVE FROM ADAM AND RESERVED HER TO BE THE MOTHER OF ALL LIVING, OR HUMANITY

God saw fit to separate Eve from Adam, and made a woman (man with a womb), or female, meaning a feminine woman. So, in Adam, were Eve and all of humanity or the fullness of humanity. Therefore, no one could come to earth without going through Adam; likewise, no one could go to heaven without going through the second or last Adam (Jesus Christ), (1 Corinthians 15:45). This is why Jesus Christ told Nicodemus that you must be born again or else you cannot see or enter into the kingdom of God, or heaven. This is also why, when God wanted to come to earth to die for the sins of mankind, the ultimate sacrifice because of Adam's sin, He came through a woman, the Virgin Mary. He came through Adam, thus taking on the form of flesh and becoming the second Adam, by which he now restores or reroutes mankind into heaven, those who are born of him.

> For since by man came death, by man came also the resurrection of the dead. For as in Adam all die, even so in Christ shall all be made alive.
>
> 1 Corinthians 15:21-21 (KJV)

Jesus Christ, through willful obedience, secured forever those who, through faith in him or acceptance in him, will become heirs of righteousness and granted them eternal life, thus bringing us back into fellowship or communion with God.

For in Adam dwells the fullness of humanity, meaning those who are and will be born of Adam and Eve. So also in Jesus Christ dwells the fullness of the Godhead bodily. Jesus Christ is the only one who possesses eternal life; thus, no one could go to heaven without going through Jesus Christ, just as no one could come to earth without being born of a woman or coming through Adam. For Scripture is clear when it says just as woman came through man, so now man comes through woman: "For as the woman is of the man, even so is the man also by the woman; but all things of God" (1 Corinthians 11:12, KJV).

So, in Adam consisted a multitude of persons, or *sperma* (meaning "seed"), the Greek word for *sperm*. *Anisogamy*, also called *heterogamy*, refers to a form of sexual reproduction involving gametes of different sizes. The smaller gamete is considered to be a male sperm cell, whereas the larger gamete is regarded as a female egg cell (http://en.wikipedia.org/wiki/Anisogamy). Yes, what I am saying is God separated in Adam the smaller gamete from the larger gamete, and with the larger gamete, he created the woman (Eve). The main processes make up sexual reproduction. *Meiosis* is the process of reducing through division, in which the number of chromosomes per cell is halved. This separation of gametes results in the second process, *fertilization*, which is simply the fusion of gametes to produce a new organism or the restoration of the original number of chromosomes (http:// en.wikipedia.org/wiki/Sexual_reproduction). Therefore, when God decided that it was not good for man to be *alone* (complete), he separated or pulled out the large gamete and reserved that for the woman. And when man and woman are joined in marriage they become one again. Thus completing one another and enabling each other to create a seed after their own kind, in their own image; through the process of fusion and fertilization of the small and large gametes. The twenty three halved chromosomes are now joined together to make forty six chromosome; thus, we have recreation or procreation by process of the two becoming one flesh. That one flesh is the seeds or offspring of the man and the woman. But this time, the woman is the one who now has the privilege of carrying life in her womb. Mankind as a whole, both man and woman, is the carrier of the human race, or all of humanity (1 Corinthians 11:12, KJV).

> And the Lord God said, "It is not good that the man should be alone; I will make him an help meet for him." And the Lord God caused a deep sleep to fall upon Adam, and he slept: and he took one of his ribs, and closed up the flesh instead thereof; And the rib, which the Lord God had taken from man, made he a woman, and brought her unto the man.
>
> Genesis 2:20-22 (KJV)

In essence, both scrotum and ovum, or simply, sperms and eggs, once existed in Adam. God separated or took out the ovum, or the larger gametes from Adam and reserved it for Eve, who became the mother of living. Adam held on to the sperms and Eve possessed the eggs, thus making them dependent on each other for procreation. Independence or isolation of man and woman would breed extinction.

THE GREATNESS OF GOD

GOD TRANSCENDS HIS CREATION

God is greater than his creations. If God was not bigger than his creation, his creation would be God. Due to a great misunderstanding of God's greatness in respect to his creation, we see that some people worship his creation rather than worshiping him. They worship God's creation by worshiping the sun, moon, stars, cows, woods, etc. Everything he created is subject to him. There is nothing bigger or smaller than him because everything exists in him, from the smallest to the biggest. That is why he is the Alpha and the Omega, the beginning and the end. Which simply means everything begins in him (A), and everything will end in him (Z). No one or nothing can exist before him, outside of him, or apart from him. The scriptures say in him we live and move and have our being (Acts 17:28, KJV). Yes, God is bigger than heaven and earth, he is a world all by himself, he is bigger than the heavens and the earth put together; that is why the whole world is in his hands. The wise man King Solomon, after building a temple in honor to God, dedicated the temple to God, and said not even the heavens of heavens can contain God, much less the temple: "But will God indeed dwell on the earth? Behold, the heaven and heaven of heavens cannot contain thee; how much less this house that I have built?" (1 Kings 8:27, KJV; See also 2 Chronicles 2:26)

That is why heaven is where his throne is, where he sits and is worshiped, and it is also where he judges all of his creation and his creatures. Earth is a footstool. It is simply a place where his foot rests as a sign of fellowship with mankind. In order for mankind to have that fellowship with him, we must humble ourselves and bow down or prostrate at his foot in humility; then he will exalt us or bid us to come into his presence (heaven), for we are not even worthy to kneel down or bow down or prostrate before him, or even untie his shoe strap.

> Thus saith the Lord, "The heaven is my throne, and the earth is my footstool: where is the house that ye build unto me? And where is the place of my rest?"
>
> Isaiah 66:1 (KJV)

> But Solomon built him a house. Howbeit the most high dwelleth not in temples made with hands; as saith the prophet, "Heaven is my throne, and earth is my footstool: what house will ye build me?" saith the Lord: or what is the place of my rest? Hath not my hand made all these things?
>
> Acts 7:47-50 (KJV)

JESUS WAS NOT CREATED; HE WAS SEPARATED

God is all knowing (omniscient); He determines the end from the beginning. Based on his foreknowledge, he determines what is going to happen even before it happens. Before the creation of heaven and earth, God knew through his foreknowledge that Lucifer, who is now called Satan, would betray him in heaven and would cause one third of the angels in heaven to follow him in rebelling against him. He knew Satan was going to deceive mankind into sinning against God, thereby causing them to indirectly and unconsciously join him in his rebellion against Him. Based on God's foreknowledge, He made provision and preparation for this entire insidious coup or treason against Him before the foundation of the world, before the creation of heaven and earth, by separating or reserving one aspect of his being; the Word of God, Jesus Christ. So God planned the end from the beginning because he knows the end from the beginning. His plan went as follows:

1. He would reserve one aspect of His being by eternally separating Him from Himself, causing a slaying for the sacrifice of mankind, thus becoming the Word of God, the same as his spoken word. He would become the very word by which God speaks or utters, and through which all things would be created and made (Genesis 1:3, KJV). As also stated:

In the beginning was the Word, and the Word was with God, and the Word was God...He was in the world, and the world was made by him, and the world knew him not.

John 1:1, 10 (KJV)

He is the Word that created light. Another example: God said he sent his Word to heal our disease, or his Word would not return to him void; He is that Word that heals all our disease.

So shall my word be that goeth forth out of my mouth: it shall not return unto me void, but it shall accomplish that which I please, and it shall prosper in the thing whereto I sent it.

Isaiah 55: 11 (KJV)

He sent his word, and healed them, and delivered them from their destructions.

Psalm 107:20 (KJV)

This is the Word of Jesus Christ, who came to deliver us from destruction, or heals our disease, and did not return to the Father without accomplishing the task given to him before the foundation of the world.

2. The Word of God was given the task, the responsibilities, and the project, to govern and oversee the restoration of mankind and to bring earth back to God's control,

3. The plan included the atonement of mankind through the shedding of blood to satisfy God's righteous requirement for forgiveness; for without the shedding of blood, there is no forgiveness of sin. So the Word of God had to incarnate to the earth's realm by temporarily relocating from heaven to earth and by restricting his deity from being born of a virgin, thus clothing himself in human form. On earth, he would be known as the Son Of God or the Son of Man, which simply means God whose Spirit took on human form; thus, we see this Jesus, whom they crucified, as having two divine natures: fully man and fully God. So as Son of God or Son of Man, and through the successfulness of the cross, or tree, through obedience; he met God's sacrificial requirement for redemption of mankind by the atoning sacrifice of the shedding of blood, for without the shedding of blood, there is no remission of sin.

   And almost all things are by the law purged with blood; and without shedding of blood is no remission.

   Hebrew 9:22 (KJV)

He fulfilled this responsibility on the cross when he said, "It is finished" (John 19:20, KJV). So, Jesus Christ, who is the Son of Man, the Son of God, the Word of God, the Angel of the Lord, was separated from God before the foundation of the world. God forgave man of their sins, but he forgives not angels that sin.

4. He was also responsible for dealing with the faith of those who rebelled against him in heaven and those who refused to accept

his redemptive plan for salvation by forever condemning them to an everlasting fire which we know as the lake of fire. These fallen angels and unrepentant men, who through the work of darkness are presently working against God by way of treason, sedition, and the constant manipulation and undermining of God's authority here on earth and of his kingdom.

> And all that dwell upon the earth shall worship him, whose names are not written in the book of life of the Lamb slain from the foundation of the world.
>
> Revelation 13:8 (KJV)

The Lamb of God, slain before the foundation of the world became the sacrificial Lamb or God, sacrificing himself as his only begotten Son for the sake of the world (mankind) by separating or pulling out Jesus Christ (God) from himself, making him the Son of God, like how Eve came out of Adam and became a woman, or simply a man with a womb. And through this woman, all of human life would come. Therefore, the womb became the symbol of life, procreation of the human race. Likewise, Jesus Christ, the Son of God is the womb for mankind's eternity, or entrance to heaven. All those who are in Jesus Christ by reason of confession and acceptance of God's plan for salvation will have eternal life. Jesus Christ is this womb for mankind, whereas all those who want to go to heaven or have an everlasting life will have to be born again, simply meaning born into heaven. And Jesus Christ is the only one that can birth us into heaven because Father God has put the life of mankind or eternity in Jesus Christ. Therefore, anyone who is in Jesus Christ has eternal life; anyone who is not in Christ does not have this hope of eternity.

> For as the Father hath life in himself; so hath he given to the Son to have life in himself; And hath given him authority to execute judgment also, because he is the Son of man.
>
> John 5:26 (KJV)

> He that believeth on the Son hath everlasting life: and he that believeth not the Son shall not see life; but the wrath of God abideth on him.
>
> John 3:36 (KJV)

Thus, God reserved one aspect of himself (Christ) by slaying or separating one aspect of himself to deal with the rebellion he foresaw before he created the heavens and the earth. He reserved Jesus, the Word of God, God from God, making him the Son of God (same nature as God), the Word of God who was in the beginning with God and was God, and Christ will be the hope for mankind's redemption for eternity. Jesus Christ became the womb for mankind, the process by which mankind could be born spiritually into heaven or the kingdom of God; thereby, the continual existence of mankind hinges upon the success of Jesus Christ on the tree (cross). Below are a few references to Jesus before creation proceeded out from the bosom of God. While on earth, he thought it not robbery to be equal with God.

> The Lord possessed me in the beginning of his way, before his works of old. I was set up from everlasting, from the beginning, or from whenever the earth was. When there were no depths, I was brought forth; when there were no fountains abounding with water. Before the mountains were settled, before the hills was I brought forth: While yet he had not made the earth, nor the fields, nor the highest part of the dust of the world. When he prepared the heavens, I was there: when he set a compass upon the face of the depth: When he established the clouds above: when he strengthened the fountains of the deep: When he gave to the sea his decree, that the waters should not pass his commandment: when he appointed the foundations of the earth: Then I was by him, as one brought up with him: and I was daily his delight, rejoicing always before

him; Rejoicing in the habitable part of his earth; and my delights were with the sons of men.

Proverb 8:22-31 (KJV)

Let this mind be in you, which was also in Christ Jesus: Who, being in the form of God, thought it not robbery to be equal with God.

Philippians 2:5 (KJV)

And now, O Father, glorify thou me with thine own self with the glory which I had with thee before the world was.

John 17: 5 (KJV)

For the Father himself loveth you, because ye have loved me, and have believed that I came out from God. I came forth from the Father, and am come into the world: again, I leave the world, and go to the Father.

John 16:27-28 (KJV)

In reference to Proverbs 8:22-31 (KJV), I just want to mention that this particular verse is used by some to state that Jesus Christ was created or brought into existence before heaven and earth were created. I briefly explain this thought in my first book, entitled *His Name Is Not God*, stating that if you study the whole text of Proverbs 8 contextually, you will see that he is talking about wisdom and how wisdom was portrayed in the mind of God before creation. I also explain that through wisdom we see the manifestation of the mind of God in creation. In this book, I take this concept a step further to say that since God knows the end from the beginning and knows what is going to happen before it happens, he made provision for mankind by reserving one aspect of his being by separating the Word of God (Jesus) from himself to deal with the fall of man and Satan and the fallen angels. Therefore, when scriptures states that the Lamb of God was slain before the foundation of the world, I understand it to be that God became the sacrificial lamb by sacrificing himself as the only begotten Son for the sake of the world (mankind). H accomplished this by separating or pulling out Jesus Christ (God) from himself; God from God, thus making him the Son of God. If we believe that Jesus Christ is God, we know that God cannot be created; therefore, Jesus Christ is uncreated.

GOD ENTERS HIS CREATION

GOD STEPPED INTO HIS CREATION, FIRST IN HEAVEN AS ANGEL OF THE LORD, SECOND ON EARTH AS SON OF GOD, OR SON OF MAN

So once Jesus Christ was begotten before creation, separated (slain) from God, he was reserved to be the sacrificial lamb that would save the world. He was now responsible for the redemption of mankind from the fall. They, or he, created the heavens and earth and all things in it. He created the heavens and set his throne there. And there He stepped into his creation in heaven as the angel of the Lord (God as angel) to rule all of creation from heaven and to be worshiped. He made angels to dwell and to worship him.

> And the angel of the Lord called unto him out of heaven, and said, Abraham, Abraham: and he said, Here am I. And he said, Lay not thine hand upon the lad, neither do thou any thing unto him: for now I know that thou fearest God, seeing thou hast not withheld thy son, thine only son from me. And Abraham lifted up his eyes, and looked, and behold behind him a ram caught in a thicket by his horns: and Abraham went and took the ram, and offered him up for a burnt offering in the stead of his son. And Abraham called the name of that place Jehovahjireh: as it is said to this day, In the mount of the LORD it shall be seen. And the angel of the LORD called unto Abraham out of heaven the second time, And said, By myself have I sworn, saith the LORD, for because thou hast done this thing, and hast not withheld thy son, thine only son: That in blessing I will bless thee, and in multiplying I

> will multiply thy seed as the stars of the heaven, and as the sand which is upon the sea shore; and thy seed shall possess the gate of his enemies; And in thy seed shall all the nations of the earth be blessed; because thou hast obeyed my voice.
>
> Genesis 22:11-18 (KJV)
See also Genesis 16:7-13 or Exodus 3:2-6 (KJV).

He created angels to dwell in his presence to worship Him; He gave them powers in ranking and in order, and he made them with indestructible abilities but he did not spare them when they sinned but casts them down to hell (2 Peter 2:4, KJV). Even though they were created with indestructible ability, only God could destroy them. God has many ways of destroying them. For one, he could *un*-create them; yes, God has the power to create and to *un*-create. But whatever reason God still allows them to wreak havoc on the earth is beyond me. Nevertheless, I trust the Lord because I know his ways are perfect; his ways are higher than mine, just as the east is far from the west and the south is far from the north, his way is higher than ours. I know for certain through the Scripture that he is going to destroy them through an everlasting fire, the lake of fire. He created the earth and everything that is in it and made man in his image and likeness, but made them a little lower than the angels, so that when they sin, they will be forgiven through the blood shed of Jesus Christ. He extended or delegated authority to mankind by giving Adam dominion over the work of his hands, over everything he created here on earth, not heaven. Then God will step into His earth the second time when the fullness of time comes as the Son of God or Son of Man (God as man), thus all of creation will answer to him in heaven whether creation likes it or not, whether they have chosen to alienate themselves from God; they still have to answer to him. All kingdoms will have to abide by his laws and give accountability to him. Whatever nation or kingdom refuses to answer to him or obey his laws, he alone reserves the rights to bring about judgment, execution, plagues, famine, or condemnation, etc., just as we see throughout Scripture; like Noah and the flood, Sodom and Gomorrah, the tower of Babel, the ten plagues in Egypt, etc.

THE OTHER DIMENSION

IS GOD A PERSON, PLACE, AND THING?

And now, O Father, glorify thou me with thine own self with the glory which I had with thee before the world was.

John 17:5 (KJV)

Here in this reference, we see Jesus asking the Father to glorify him with the glory; He and the father had before heaven and earth's creation, when nothing was in existence, and there only existed God. This existence is a dimension outside of heaven and earth, a place that cannot be phantom, the only realm of existence without a beginning. This dimension or realm has not been spoken of, because it cannot be conceived of; it is a realm where the essence of God, the nature of God, and the personhood of God (Godhead) is one. In fact, one can conclude that God is a person, a place, and a thing, all at once, which some will say is the definition of a noun or even pantheism. This dimension or realm of existence is where the source of all life, light, and love flows from. This dimension is called by Jesus Christ the unapproachable light, which no one has entered or gone there, only he who came from there (1 Timothy 6:16, KJV). This dimension is what holds together the heavens and the earth and makes it possible for heaven and earth to continue to exist. This dimension is higher than the heavens; this dimension is what is presently giving light to heaven, just as the sun gives light to the earth. In heaven, where there is no sun or moon, this light is the glory of God. God was not in heaven or earth when he created the heavens and the earth; in fact, it was through this dimension that God created the heavens and the earth and all things visible and invisible. This realm of existence or dimension does not have a beginning, nor will it have an end. Scripture attests to this fact that in him we live, move, and have our being. It is also a fact that Jesus Christ spoke the truth when explained that the heavens and the earth will pass away but his words, will not. Equally truthful was his declaration that the heaven and the earth will be rolled up like a scroll but his word will not fail. Only in this dimension could a person ascribe the word *pantheism* to God. Pantheism is a belief that the physical universe is equivalent to God and that there is no division between the creator and the substance of its creation; therefore God is creation. I believe that only in this dimension is the theory of pantheism true. What I am describing could be a person, place, and thing (pantheism), for we know that the creation of heaven and earth is subject to God. Only in this dimension or realm could it be possible that God is one with his creation. But as far as the heavens and the earth, God is greater than both the heaven and earth put together (Pan-en-theism). Pan-en-theism is also a belief that creation, or the physical universe, is joined to God and yet God is greater than the material universe. Pandeism is an alternative belief that God preceded the universe and created it, but is now equivalent with it, which cannot be true because whatever God created will always be subject to God. This realm of existence I describe is uncreated; this dimension is God. This brings me to another word, *deism*, which is a belief that there is a God who created all things, but this God does not intervene with his creation because he put law in place to deal with that. So therefore they don't believe in prophecy, miracles, supernatural power, revelation, etc.; they only believe in reasoning and observation of the physical world. These are our everyday scientists, intellectuals, philosophers, astronomers, sociologists who adhere to this theory, etc. The danger of this belief eradicates the hope of redemption and all that Jesus came to do for us to propel us back into proper fellowship with God. This belief sprang up in the early eighteenth century, during the age of enlightenment. Our founding fathers were deists when they came from Europe to the new world, and it was with this belief that they established the United States of America. This is the belief that presently runs the world; a world of intellectuals who have alienated God and indirectly or directly embraced these ancient evil spirits that promised them world power, world success, wealth, money, etc., as long as they do his bidding. And as a result, they have been advancing the devil's kingdom by extending and merging the kingdom of Satan and the kingdom of men. So don't be surprised if you see demonic activities in the world and yet mankind seems oblivious to it all.

BEFORE THE FALL

> This I say then, walk in the Spirit, and ye shall not fulfill the lust of the flesh.
>
> Galatians 5:16 (KJV)

Before the fall of Adam and Eve, earth was under God's jurisdiction. When God created the heavens and the earth and all things in it; heaven and earth were under one kingdom, under the kingdom of God. He also planted a beautiful garden in the east of Eden, and there he put man, whom he created and formed in his image and likeness. God then delegated authority to the man on earth by giving him dominion over everything he had created on earth. This garden was also called the garden of God (Ezekiel 28:13, KJV). It was a spiritual garden or a spiritual place here on earth; described by many as a paradise. In order to live in this garden or access this paradise, you must be a spiritual being or a person that walks and lives in the spirit; this was the state or condition of Adam and Eve before the sin. You see, before Adam and Eve sinned, their eyes were only open to the spiritual realm. That is why the scripture states that the man and his wife were naked and not ashamed (Genesis 2:25, KJV). Why were they not ashamed? *Naked* in this sense meant that they were present before God without hindrance, without guilt, and without any shame. They were as babies or toddlers before their maker, and they were not conscious of their nakedness or nudity. They were not conscious about self; they were only conscious about God, their spiritual Father. It was when they ate the forbidden fruit that they gained knowledge of self, or selfishness, or low self-esteem. This garden of Eden is the spiritual dimension between heaven and earth. This is why it cannot be located and cannot been seen with the natural eyes; nor can it be occupied with the natural or physical body. In order to see or enter the garden of Eden, this spiritual dimension, you must walk and live in the spirit, through the process of Jesus Christ, opening up your spiritual eyes to see the kingdom of God, like he told Nicodemus in John 3:1-8. To get a good grasp of this garden, think of Jesus' transfiguration. Here within the mount of transfiguration, we saw Jesus Christ step into a spiritual dimension; his face became shining like the sun; his raiment became exceedingly white, and there appeared to him Moses and Elijah, talking with Jesus. Then a voice from heaven stated, "This is my beloved Son. In him I am well pleased (Matthew 17:5, KJV)." Moses is the representation of the law, Elijah represents the prophets, and Jesus Christ represents the fulfillment of both the law and prophets; he also fulfilled the Psalms (Matthew 17:1-5, KJV).

> I, John, who also am your brother, and companion in tribulation, and in the kingdom and patience of Jesus Christ, was in the isle that is called Patmos, for the Word of God, and for the testimony of Jesus Christ. I was in the Spirit on the Lord's Day, and heard behind me a great voice, as of a trumpet.
>
> Revelation 1:9-10 (KJV)

This Garden of Eden or paradise represented:

A. The presence of God here on earth.

B. Where man once knew God.

C. Where God walked, talked, supped, and communed with man.

D. When man was governor by their spirit and not their flesh.

E. While in the spirit, man could see the spiritual realm or look up into the heavens and join in with the angels in worship to God, and see God high and lifted on his throne.

F. In this garden of Eden, men were not aging or growing old; if they were aging, they would have grown old and died.

G. In this garden, Adam and Eve had the ability to talk with animals.

H. The garden was not confined to time; it was a timeless place, just like heaven.

I. The garden was an extension of heaven on earth.

Adam was first created and then formed. When we say *created*, we are simply saying that Adam's spirit was created. God first created the spirit of man, or Adam.

> And God said, Let us make man in our image, after our likeness: and let them have dominion over the fish of the sea, and over the fowl of the air, and over the cattle, and over all the earth, and every creeping thing that creepeth upon the earth.
>
> Genesis 1:26 (KJV)

Then he formed the body from the dust of the ground for the spirit he had created.

> And the Lord God formed man of the dust of the ground, and breathed into his nostrils the breath of life; and man became a living soul.
>
> Genesis 2:7 (KJV)

Then the spirit that was created in Genesis 1:26 (KJV) was breathed into the dust or clay, which was formed from the ground in Genesis 2:7 (KJV), and as a result, man, or Adam, became alive, or a living soul. How did I conclude this analysis? If you read Genesis 2:1-5

(KJV), you see that the heavens and the earth and all the host of them were finished, and God rested from all his work and blessed the seventh day. We also see the history of heaven and earth before any plant of the field was on the earth or before any herb of the field had grown because God had not caused it to rain upon the earth and there was no man to till the ground. The question one must ask is why was there not man on the earth to till the ground if man was created in Genesis 1:26 (KJV). It only makes sense if we conclude that the spirit of man was created in Genesis 1:26 (KJV), and the flesh of man was formed in Genesis 2:7, and he put or breathed into the formed man, the spirit he had created in Genesis 1:26, and as a result, man became a living soul. In fact, let me reference this scripture so you don't think I'm making this up.

> Thus the heavens and the earth were finished, and all the host of them.
> And on the seventh day, God ended his work which he had made; and he rested on the seventh day from all his work which he had made. And God blessed the seventh day, and sanctified it: because that in it he had rested from all his work which God created and made. These are the generations of the heavens and of the earth when they were created, in the day that the LORD God made the earth and the heavens, And every plant of the field before it was in the earth, and every herb of the field before it grew: for the LORD God had not caused it to rain upon the earth, and there was not a man to till the ground. But there went up a mist from the earth, and watered the whole face of the ground. And the LORD God formed man of the dust of the ground, and breathed into his nostrils the breath of life; and man became a living soul.
>
> > Genesis 2:1-7 (KJV)

Adam and Eve were created as spiritual beings and clothed in human form (flesh or dust), and they lived and dwelled in the spiritual realm until they sinned by disobeying God their creator and by obeying the voice of the creature (Satan), who is cursed forever. As a result of their disobedience, their spirits died; meaning they no longer lived and walked in the spirit, nor were they God conscious; thus, they severed their relationship with God. They lost the spiritual sense that enabled them to directly communicate with God. They became conscious of self, no longer able to live in the garden of Eden; no longer able to walk in the spirit or see into the spirit. In essence, they became spiritually blinded or dead. As a result of their disobedience, they were immediately driven or evicted out of the garden of Eden or paradise to earth where they were formed were also Satan and his demons were banished or exiled to. Through their disobedience, they lost their spiritual connection with God; the connection that made it possible to live in the spirit (spiritual realm); the connection that made it possible to live in the garden or paradise; this connection is the Holy Spirit. The Holy Spirit made it possible to live in the presence of God. They lost everything that the garden represented. For example, instead of being governed by the spirit, they were now governed by the flesh; instead living forever, they were no longer immortal, but became mortal and is now have an appointed time with death (Hebrew 9:27, KJV). Instead of staying young and strong, they grew old and weak. Instead of being able to communicate with animals, they slowly lost their connection with animals. In essence, they became mortal, liable or subject to death. There was a spiritual void and the flesh or Satan began to fill that void; as a result, we clearly see the manifestation of the fruits of the flesh throughout the course of man's history which are envy, murder, dissention, adultery, fornication, drunkenness, witchcraft, adultery, etc. All of these are the fruits and manifestation of the devil and his demons, and since men have lost their connection or Holy Spirit, they obey or are influenced by the devil and his demonic forces. God promised that those who produce such fruits will not enter his kingdom.

> Now the works of the flesh are manifest, which are these: adultery, fornication, uncleanness, lasciviousness, idolatry, witchcraft, hatred, variance, emulations, wrath, strife, seditions, heresies, envy, murder, drunkenness, reveling, and such like, of the which I tell you before, as I have also told you in time past, that they which do such things shall not inherit the kingdom of God.
>
> Galatians 5:19-22

And the influence of the flesh and work of the flesh is under the control of no other than Satan and his demons. The garden of Eden or paradise was a spiritual realm or place; it was something like the mount of transfiguration, when Jesus took three of his disciples, Peter, James, and John to the top of the mountain and opened up their eyes and they saw Jesus Christ transfigured in front of them and saw Moses and Elijah speaking to Jesus, their master. This transfiguration the Lord Jesus Christ privileged Peter, James, and John to see and witness by opening their spiritual eyes is a result of being able to walk and live in the spirit.

Let me give you another example or reference of being able to see into the spiritual realm. Remember when the Syrian army surrounded Elisha the prophet, as he warned the King of Israel of the Syrian plans of ambush. The king of Syria was so frustrated that he thought there were spies among his soldiers and one of his servants said that the prophet Elisha told what the king spoke in his bedroom to the king of Israel. So they surrounded Elisha and his servant's house to kill them. And Elisha prayed to God and asked that He open his servant's eyes so that he would see that there are more with them then against them. And when God opened up the servant's eyes, he saw hosts of God's army with chariots.

And when the servant of the man of God was risen early, and gone forth, behold, an host compassed the city both with horses and chariots. And his servant said unto him, Alas, my master! How shall we do? And he answered, Fear not: for they that be with us are more than they that be with them. And Elisha prayed, and said, LORD, I pray thee, open his eyes, that he may see. And the LORD opened the eyes of the young man; and he saw: and, behold, the mountain was full of horses and chariots of fire round about Elisha. And when they came down to him, Elisha prayed unto the LORD, and said, smite this people, I pray thee, with blindness. And he smote them with blindness according to the word of Elisha.

2 kings 6:15-18 (KJV)

KINGS AND KINGDOMS

THREE TYPES OF KINGDOMS

The following discussion will set the stage for the rest of the chapters. In this discussion, we will learn that there are four types of kingdoms; the kingdom of God, the kingdom of Satan, the kingdom of men and the animal kingdom. For the sake of argument, I will only be discussing three of these kingdoms. The kingdom of God is a kingdom in which God is the righteous, sovereign king; the kingdom of Satan is a kingdom in which Satan is the unrighteous king, and the kingdom of men is a kingdom in which man is the king. The kingdom of Satan seeks to oppose and counteract God's kingdom and the influence he has over the kingdom of men, thereby making the kingdom of men an anti-God kingdom. The kingdom of men is desperately seeking to be an atheistic kingdom, by which it seeks to be an autonomous government, free of any influences, free from either the kingdom of God or the kingdom of Satan. This is one of the reasons why mankind is slowly stripping the title God out of the schools, constitutions, courts, laws, etc. This concept will never work because both kingdoms are superior over the kingdom of men and both kingdoms will always influence the kingdom of men. God's kingdom seeks to rule the kingdom of men in righteousness and the kingdom of Satan seeks to rule the kingdom of men in unrighteousness and destruction; therefore, there is a spiritual warfare that is being fought every day over the children of the kingdom of men and the one that wins is determined by the yielding of the will of mankind to that kingdom. This warfare is conducted one individual at a time, or through influential individuals that will persuade or coerce mankind into submitting to the God or a false god. Therefore, the individual either becomes a part of God's family; the kingdom of God or part of Satan's slaves, the kingdom of Satan. God is the sovereign judge and king over all his creation and kingdoms; he does not need the obedience of men to accomplish his purpose or will. Because he is the one that created the hearts of men, he is the one who hardens or softens men's hearts for his purpose, just as he did with the pharaoh king of Egypt. Therefore, God is simply going to come to earth in the form of a man (Jesus) to establish his kingdom on earth and destroy all other kingdoms, which will once and for all restore earth back to his control like the way it was before Adam and Eve forfeited their dominion to Satan. And all those that will not yield to him or his kingdom, he will destroy. An atheistic kingdom is the concept whereby the kingdom of men wants to be self-governed, desiring to be its own god. This was the reason of Satan's offer to mankind (Adam and Eve), when the devil deceived Eve by telling her that she would become like God, knowing good and evil (Genesis 3:5, KJV). But just as the kingdom of Satan is subjected to God, so is the kingdom of men; both kingdom will always be subjected to God, the Creator of the universe, until God destroys both of these kingdoms and recreates or restores the kingdom of men back to authority.

Because both the kingdom of Satan and kingdom of men are subject to God, Satan seeks partnership and unity with the kingdom of men. Satan believes that this partnership will give him more power and numbers to battle against God and the coming judgment of Satan and mankind. So, Satan and his demons are contracting men and preparing them for the coming war; he is making promises to them that those who submit to him and yield to his bidding; he will grant them power; give them wealth and share his glory, his throne with mankind. I know this fact to be true because he tried that with Jesus Christ and Jesus told him to get thee behind him and he rebuked him.

> Again, the devil taketh him up into an exceeding high mountain, and sheweth him all the kingdoms of the world, and the glory of them…
>
> Matthew 4:8-10 (KJV)

But it is sad to say that there are those who have submitted to Satan's accolades, including the temptation for money, wealth, power, etc., and are now employed or working for Satan's kingdom; these individuals or groups or government works are in cahoots with the kingdom of Satan in advancing his kingdom. This unity or partnership with the kingdom of Satan has given Satan legal rights to rule mankind through governments, prime ministers, senators, songs, rappers, false churches, mass, etc. by rewriting laws that oppose the universal laws of God. But regardless of any attempt to alienate God, God's kingdom rules and overrides all others.

Both the kingdom of Satan and the kingdom of men, regardless of joint venture, must answer to the kingdom of God. They must abide by God's rules and regulations. When they don't or refuse, he destroys them, deposing their kingdom or removing and replacing the king. The book of Daniel gives us a glimpse of this reality:

> Then was the secret revealed unto Daniel in a night vision. Then Daniel blessed the God of heaven. Daniel answered and said, Blessed be the name of God for ever and ever: for wisdom and might are his: And he changeth the times and the seasons: he removeth kings, and setteth up kings: he giveth wisdom unto the wise, and knowledge to them that know understanding:
>
> Daniel 2:19-21 (KJV)

Therefore, the kingdom of God is sovereign over all other kingdoms and is regulated by him; he exalts and deposes any kingdom at his pleasure. The kingdom of God is the only true kingdom that will last forever and in due time he will destroy all other kingdoms and restore earth to its rightful place as it was before the fall of mankind, under his rule, under his kingdom. Therefore, it is safe to conclude that the kingdom of Satan and his influences over the kingdom of men is a temporary and counterfeit kingdom.

WHAT CONSTITUTES A KING OR KINGDOM?

Who is a king? And what is a kingdom? In order to understand these concepts, we have to: (1), understand it from God's perspective or from the inception of the very first kingdom, the kingdom of heaven. To understand God's viewpoint, we must look at the biblical record that illustrates God's perspective. And (2), we have to review what heaven and earth were like before the rebellion in heaven and the fall of Adam and Eve (mankind) on earth, which resulted in the creation of two counterfeit kingdoms, the kingdom of Satan and the kingdom of men. God is the one and only king over all of creation. So let's take this journey by looking at the conditions of heaven and earth under God's kingdom before earth became separated from God's kingdom. Understanding the conditions of heaven and earth before its isolation, alienation or separation from God will demonstrate the general rules of how a king governed a kingdom. Before the rebellion in heaven and the disobedience on earth, there were standards that dictated how a king and his kingdom should operate. This approach sets the standard, gives us a blueprint of what a king and his kingdom should be like. Previewing the kingdom of God gives us the knowledge to know the difference between a real king and his kingdom and the counterfeit kings and kingdoms and will also equip us to know what constitutes a king and his kingdom. The dictionary defines a king as a male sovereign; ruler of a kingdom, and a kingdom as a domain in which something is dominant; a country with a king as head of state. A true king must possess at least five to six of these traits with the exception of the first one, because no king can possess that quality to be the king of heaven, unless they are God:

A. He must be a creator; this is why God is king over heaven and earth—because he created it.

B. He must be a visionary, have the ability to see things before they happen and act on it to prevent loss or harm to anyone who is following him or her. A leader or a king without a vision endangers those who are following him; their end will be destruction.

C. He must have a territory or domain: the Kingdom of Heaven

D. He must have a throne where he can administer judgments.

> But the Lord shall endure for ever: he hath prepared his throne for judgment.
> And he shall judge the world in righteousness, he shall minister judgment to the people in uprightness.
>
> Psalm 9:7-8 (KJV)

E. He must have an army or military to protect its people from war-

> And the Lord shall utter his voice before his army: for his camp is very great: for he is strong that executeth his word: for the day of the Lord is great and very terrible; and who can abide it?
>
> Joel 2:11 (KJV)

F. And the king must love its citizens or people because you won't protect or sacrifice yourself if you do not love your people or citizens.

> For God so loved the world, that he gave his only begotten Son, that whosoever believeth in him should not perish, but have everlasting life.
>
> John 3:16 (KJV)

Without a king, there cannot be a kingdom, for a kingdom is a reflection of the king. This concept is true in the kingdom of God; this is why the *kingdom of God* and the *kingdom of heaven* are used interchangeably throughout biblical record or Scripture. Because everything that is God mirrors his kingdom. Therefore, a king is one who rules over a kingdom and a kingdom is the specific territory or domain of a king. The question is, how does one become a king or a ruler over a specific territory or domain? The first rule is that the one who created it or fathered it is automatically king and lord over all of it; thus, in the beginning, God created the heavens and the earth. This is also why he alone qualifies to be called the only wise king or King of kings. Second, the king reserves all the rights to do whatever he deems necessary with his kingdom with no apology; he can delegate a certain portion of his kingdom to whom he pleases, as was the case when He gave Adam dominion (power or authority) over all of earth. Another good example would be when pharaoh made Joseph ruler over his entire household and all of Egypt.

> Thou shalt be over my house, and according unto thy word shall all my people be ruled: only in the throne will I be greater than thou. And Pharaoh said unto Joseph, See, I have set thee over all the land of Egypt. And Pharaoh took off his ring from his hand, and put it upon Joseph's hand, and arrayed him in vestures of fine linen, and put a gold chain about his neck;
>
> Genesis 41:40-42 (KJV)

Third, he alone reserves all the right, without any apology, to choose who he wants in his kingdom. Yes, God's kingdom is a form of monarchy; he has supreme and absolute power because he lives forever and his power is never distributed. God's kingdom is not a democratic kingdom or a democratic government where power is lodged in the people, who in turn, through a majority, choose a king or a representative. As an example, in my house, and even in your house, no one can come through your front door without an invitation. So why are you trying to force yourself in God's kingdom without accepting his invitation? Do you know that heaven is the Father's house?

> Let not your heart be troubled: ye believe in God, believe also in me. In my Father's house are many mansions: if it were not so, I would have told you. I go to prepare a place for you. And if I go and prepare a place for you, I will come again, and receive you unto myself; that where I am, there ye may be also.
>
> John 14:1-3 (KJV)

In God's kingdom, the king is the one that chooses you or does all the choosing as to who can come into his kingdom that he has prepared or created.

> Ye have not chosen me, but I have chosen you, and ordained you, that ye should go and bring forth fruit, and that your fruit should remain: that whatsoever ye shall ask of the Father in my name, he may give it you.
>
> John 15:16 (KJV)

Just so that he is fair and not biased in determining who may enter his kingdom of heaven, he provide us the Ten Commandments– his minimum standards that guide us to heaven. And when he saw that we were still unable to live up to his minimum standards, he came down from heaven as the Son of God in the personhood of Jesus Christ to prove to us that it can be done by teaching us and simplifying or summarizing the Ten Commandment into the two great commandments.

> And one of the scribes came, and having heard them reason together, and perceive that he had answered them well, asked him, "Which is the first commandment of all?" And Jesus answered him, "The first of all the commandments is, Hear, O Israel; The Lord our God is one Lord: And thou shalt love the Lord thy God with all thy heart, and with all thy soul, and with all thy mind, and with all thy strength: this is the first commandment. And the second is like, namely this, Thou shalt love thy neighbour as thyself. There is none other commandment greater than these. And the scribe said unto him, Well, Master, thou hast said the truth: for there is one God; and there is none other but he: And to love him with all the heart, and with all the understanding, and with all the soul, and with all the strength, and to love his neighbour as himself, is more than all whole burnt offerings and sacrifices.
>
> Mark 12:28-33 (KJV)

Once Jesus saw that we still could not make it, that we kept falling short of his commandments, he gave us grace by sacrificing himself on the cross or tree in our place and thus paid the righteous penalty of sin. So the law could no longer condemn us and thus became our righteousness, meaning he will be the one to judge and condemn us, because he has paid the price for our sins.

> I do not frustrate the grace of God: for if righteousness come by the law, then Christ is dead in vain.
>
> Galatians 2:21 (KJV)

The only commandment he now asks of us is to simply believe that he is the Son of God (John 3:16-17). Nevertheless, if you fall short of his commandment, just believe in his Son Jesus Christ and believe in your heart that he died for your sins, and you will be saved from your sin. Know that he will grant you access into his kingdom unless you have your own heaven that you put put yourself into. He also promises that those who by reason come to believe in him and seek to live right before him, not only will be granted access into his kingdom, but will also be provided everlasting life.

A kingdom is a direct result of what the king is; therefore, a kingdom must be a reflection of the king. What do I mean by that? What I'm saying is, when a king is in power, everything he is will become a reflection or will be mirrored by his kingdom. If he is a righteous king, the people or the kingdom will experience righteousness or, for lack of better terms, right living. The kingdom will experience peace, wealth, abundance, prosperity, etc., just as he himself lavishes on these things within his palace. But if he is wicked, everything he is will also bleed into his kingdom, causing a great outcry from the people for his ungodly nature and unjust rulership. The wicked king or ruler will burden the people and impose unnecessary behavior that violates sound government that is opposite of the wishes of people and God. Within his kingdom, the wicked are rewarded instead of punished, and injustice runs rampant because of authority being granted to a wicked ruler: "When the righteous are in authority, the people rejoice: but when the wicked beareth rule, the people mourn" (Proverbs 29:2 KJV).

When the wicked rules, he indirectly releases a spirit of wickedness throughout the kingdom; thus evil begets evil, wicked attracts wickedness, and unlawful activities is practiced without any fear of God, who is judge of all kings and kingdoms. The opposite is true when the righteous are in authority; they release the spirit of righteousness throughout the kingdom, and that spirit attracts all those who are righteous that will aid him to established a righteous kingdom. This is why it is so important that we prudently and carefully select our leaders. We see a glimpse of this truth throughout Scripture. As we examine the leadership of the kings of the Israel, we see that when the righteous governed, there was always peace, abundance of wealth, prosperity and true worship to the God and creator of heaven and earth. The opposite is also true; when the wicked rule, we see hunger, adultery, false worship, famine, wars, captivity, injustices, wars, etc. The books of 1 and 2 Samuel, 1 and 2 Kings, and also 1 Chronicles provide insight to these truths. As you examine these books, you will see the nature and circumstances of the children of Israel and the results of a righteous or wicked king.

The concept of a righteous kingdom was evident when all of creation was under God's rulership. Heaven and earth was one kingdom under God; it was very fruitful and productive, and all that he is, was reflected by his kingdom. There was no lack, as was evident when God put Adam in the garden of Eden to dress it, which was the garden of God. All of creation was in harmony; including angels, men, and animals. They all lived as one in peace and love. God's kingdom did not have hunger, famine, sickness, disease, death, homelessness, starvation, etc. This kingdom was possible because he is righteous. The kingdom of heaven is probably two, three, four, five, etc. times bigger than earth; regardless there is only one king over that vast kingdom. It is not divided into country, nation, or region like the kingdom of men is, where every county, nation, and region has its own king. In a world where there are divisions of kings and kingdoms, there will always be war, invasion, and imperialism, because one king will always feel a need to expand his power, kingdom or government by waging war or invading another territory or domain.

Therefore, only God can bring about total peace, free of war, hunger, famine, homelessness, death, sickness, and disease, to this world. All who try to establish any kingdom apart from God, the only wise King, I promise will fall short; thus, says the Word of God.

When earth was isolated from God's domain, the authority or dominion that was delegated or extended to Adam was forfeited to Satan through deception. Thus, earth was now in rebellion, and as a result, earth was removed from under the kingdom of God because there was no longer a representation of God on earth. Adam and Eve had turned their back on God and started to follow Satan; as the Scripture says, who you obey is who you will serve: "Know ye not, that to whom ye yield yourselves servants to obey, his servants ye are to whom ye obey; whether of sin unto death, or of obedience unto righteousness?" (Roman 6:16, KJV)

This act of sedition by Satan and his fallen angels through the willful participation of Adam brought about a deviation from the kingdom of God. This deviation resulted in two other kingdoms: the kingdom of Satan and the kingdom of men.

THE KINGDOM OF GOD

> Thy kingdom come, Thy will be done in earth, as it is in heaven.
>
> Matthew 6:10 (KJV)

King of all kings, kingdom of all kingdoms, the only wise King, Creator of all things—thrones, dominion, powers, principalities, heaven, and earth—ruler and Lord of all the earth. His name is Jesus, the King of God's kingdom. He satisfies all the requirements to be the king of heaven. He was the Word with God in the beginning, and He created the heavens and the earth and all things:

> All things were made by him; and without him was not any thing made that was made.
>
> John 1:3 (KJV)

> He has a throne were he will administer judgment and will judge all people.
> Thy throne, O God, is forever and ever: the sceptre of thy kingdom is a right sceptre.
>
> Psalm 45:6 (KJV)

> But unto the Son he saith, Thy throne, O God, is forever and ever: a sceptre of righteousness is the sceptre of thy kingdom;
>
> Hebrew 1:8 (KJV)

As also said that we will all appear at the judgment seat of Jesus Christ, and Jesus Christ will judge everyone according to his righteousness.

> For we must all appear before the judgment seat of Christ; that everyone may receive the things done in his body, according to that he hath done, whether it be good or bad.
>
> 2 Corinthians 5:10 (KJV)

God, through his wisdom, will restore earth back to his kingdom or rulership. He announced to King David through the prophet Nathan that he would establish his kingdom through his throne on earth forever (2 Samuel 7:1-13, KJV). This kingdom will be an extension of heaven on earth where he will come from heaven to earth to establish his kingdom over earth; and he as the only true king will sit on the throne of King David forever. All those who are obedient to him will he give earth as their inheritance, once he defeats all kings and topples their kingdoms, including the democratic government which will engage in a fierce war against Jesus Christ the King of kings and his armies. The influence that God was going to have over the kings of Israel until he comes and sits on his throne is what we called a theocratic kingdom, or a government where God influences the kingdom of men to establish his will on earth. Likewise, any other government that is influenced by false gods or deities, will also be influenced by a theocratic government. For the throne or kingdom of David, it will be the true God, creator of heaven and earth, that will influence his kingdom forever. King David was a man after God's heart; God knows that David was a typical man who truly loved him and dedicated all his life to seeking to please God. David, when he was wrong or when he made a mistake, was quick to repent and plead for forgiveness especially when confronted, unlike the average man who when they are wrong or confronted about their error still continue in their sin. God finds stubborn people difficult to deal with. This was truth with the children of Israel; despite constantly warning about their error, they still continued to sin against God, regardless of his loving mercy and forgiveness toward them. However, this kingdom that God would establish would not require human participation for their involvement would obstruct God's purpose. God just wanted a human representative that he could come through to establish this kingdom; in return, he will protect that government or kingdom and give them victory from all who seek their destruction. Thus, the kingdom of Israel was born. This kingdom was contingent on their obedience to him. Whenever they did not obey and went after other gods, God would warn them through his prophets and remind them of their covenant with him. When they didn't repent and continued in their error, he would remove his protection or covering and let their enemies deal with them by killing them, taking some in captivity and simply driving them out of the land he swore to give to them, leaving it desolate. The kingdom of Israel was established when the children of Israel or the twelve tribes of Israel wanted to have their own physical king like all the other nations. So, they came to the prophet Samuel and said to him, "You are getting old and your two sons are not walking in your footsteps; they are corrupt, and we will not have them be our judge. So make for us a king like all the other nations." This request really displeased Samuel, because the children of Israel were indirectly rejecting God as their king. Samuel did not want to go to God and tell them what the children of Israel wanted, so God came to Samuel and told him to give the people what they wanted for they had not rejected him but had rejected God as king over them.

> And it came to pass, when Samuel was old, that he made his sons judges over Israel. Now the name of his firstborn was Joel; and the name of his second, Abiah: they were judges in Beersheba. And his sons walked not in his ways, but turned aside after lucre, and took bribes, and perverted judgment. Then all the elders of Israel gathered themselves together, and came to Samuel unto Ramah, and said unto him, Behold, thou art old, and thy sons walk not in thy ways: now make us a king to judge us like all the nations. But the thing displeased Samuel, when they said, give us

a king to judge us. And Samuel prayed unto the LORD. And the LORD said unto Samuel, hearken unto the voice of the people in all that they say unto thee: for they have not rejected thee, but they have rejected me, that I should not reign over them. According to all the works which they have done since the day that I brought them up out of Egypt even unto this day, wherewith they have forsaken me, and served other gods, so do they also unto thee.

1 Samuel 8:1-8 (KJV)

God, who is rich in mercy and faithfulness, permitted the will of the people by allowing Samuel to set up a king over them. God, however, cautioned them to make sure they were certain they wanted a king to rule over them and that they understand what they were asking for. Therefore, God outlined for them the manner of a king (1 Samuel 8:9-17 KJV):

1. He will take your sons and appoint them for himself, for his chariots and to be his horsemen; and some shall run before his chariots. (Security services or guards)
2. And he will appoint him captains over thousands and captains over fifties; and will set them to ear his ground and to reap his harvest and to make his instruments of war and instruments of his chariots. (Branches of the military)
3. And he will take your daughters to be confectionaries and to be cooks and to be bakers. (Maids or servants)
4. And he will take your fields and your vineyards and your olive yards, even the best of them and give them to his servants. (eminent domain)
5. And he will take the tenth of your seed and of your vineyards and give to his officers and to his servants. (tax-payer money)
6. And he will take your menservants and your maidservants and your goodliest young men and your asses and put them to his work.

7. He will take the tenth of your sheep: and ye shall be his servants. (Taxes)

The people, through their stubbornness, said, "Yes, we agree with all the criteria of a king," and demanded for Samuel to make them a king to judge over them. This king would protect God's people and would fight all of the children of Israel's wars. Though they had rejected God as King of Israel, he would use this kingdom to establish his everlasting kingdom, and his Son (Jesus Christ) will sit on this throne forever. Thus, Saul became Israel's first king; however, his ways displeased God, so instead of his sons inheriting the kingdom, or the kingdom being passed to his son, Jonathan, God sought out a man after his own heart to rule his people. King David became the second king because his obedience to God pleased him. And so God promised David that he would always have his seed or descendant on his throne; thus we have the concept of Jesus Christ labelled as the Son of David who is going to sit on his father's throne forever. This is what we called a theocratic kingdom or government when God influenced the kingdom or government of Israel. This kingdom on earth is ultimately going to become a kingdom where God, as the righteous King, rules over all the kingdom of men. Therefore, the kingdom of God on earth is when the King of heaven (Jesus Christ) incarnated by taking on human form to teach about his coming kingdom and the way of righteousness and all who obey him, he will extend an invitation to be a part of his kingdom. The establishment of the kings of Israel or of the twelve tribes of Israel did not go well because these kings turned from following God to worshiping other gods. As a result, the nation of Israel as a whole only had three kings that governed them; it was King Saul, King David, and King Solomon. After King Solomon, the kingdom of Israel was split into two kingdoms: the northern kingdom called Israel and the southern kingdom called Judah. The northern kingdom was comprised of ten tribes of Israel and the southern kingdom was made of the two remaining kingdoms. These two tribes were the tribe of Judah and the tribe of Benjamin. The northern kingdom which was the kings of Israel had in total twenty kings; and all of them were wicked. Likewise, the southern kingdom, which was Judah, had about twenty kings, and only seven were good; the rest were wicked. The seven good kings of Judah were King Asa, King Joash, King Amaziah, King Uzziah, King Jotham, King Hezekiah, and King Josiah. These were the good kings of the southern kingdom who yielded to the influence of God for guidance and protection.

It was during the third year of King Jehoiakim's reign, that a wicked ruler, Nebuchadnezzar, king of Babylon, came unto Jerusalem and besieged it (Daniel 1:1, KJV). God gave Jehoiakim, king of Judah into his hand with part of the vessel of the house of God, which he carried into the land of Shinar to the house of his god. And King Nebuchadnezzar spoke unto Asphpenaz, the master of his eunuchs that he should bring some of the children of Israel and of the king's seed and of the princes' children in whom there was no blemish but were well favored and skillful in all wisdom, knowledge, and understanding of science and were able to stand in the king's palace and whom they might teach the learning and the tongue of the Chaldeans (Daniel 1:2-4, KJV). Among those captives were Daniel, Hananiah, Mishael, and Azariah. While in captivity, God revealed to Daniel his plan to destroy all other kingdoms and establish his kingdom in the latter times. In the book of Daniel, we see that King Nebuchadnezzar had a dream concerning the kingdom of men in the latter times. King Nebuchadnezzar was puzzled by the purpose of this dream. And so God revealed the interpretation of the dream to his prophet, Daniel. Let's read and examine the interpretation of the dream and see how it applies to the kingdom of God:

> Daniel answered in the presence of the king, and said, the secret which the king hath demanded cannot the wise men, the astrologers, the magicians, the soothsayers, shew unto the king; But there is a God in heaven that revealeth

secrets, and maketh known to the king Nebuchadnezzar what shall be in the latter days. Thy dream, and the visions of thy head upon thy bed, are these; As for thee, O king, thy thoughts came into thy mind upon thy bed, what should come to pass hereafter: and he that revealeth secrets maketh known to thee what shall come to pass. But as for me, this secret is not revealed to me for any wisdom that I have more than any living, but for their sakes that shall make known the interpretation to the king, and that thou mightest know the thoughts of thy heart. Thou, O king, sawest, and behold a great image. This great image, whose brightness was excellent, stood before thee; and the form thereof was terrible. This image's head was of fine gold, his breast and his arms of silver, his belly and his thighs of brass, His legs of iron, his feet part of iron and part of clay. Thou sawest till that a stone was cut out without hands, which smote the image upon his feet that were of iron and clay, and brake them to pieces. Then was the iron, the clay, the brass, the silver, and the gold, broken to pieces together, and became like the chaff of the summer threshing floors; and the wind carried them away, that no place was found for them: and the stone that smote the image became a great mountain, and filled the whole earth. This is the dream; and we will tell the interpretation thereof before the king. Thou, O king, art a king of kings: for the God of heaven hath given thee a kingdom, power, and strength, and glory. And wheresoever the children of men dwell, the beasts of the field and the fowls of the heaven hath he given into thine hand, and hath made thee ruler over them all. Thou art this head of gold. And after thee shall arise another kingdom inferior to thee, and another third kingdom of brass, which shall bear rule over all the earth. And the fourth kingdom shall be strong as iron: forasmuch as iron breaketh in pieces and subdueth all things: and as iron that breaketh all these, shall it break in pieces and bruise.

> Daniel 2:27-40 (KJV)

As we examine Daniel's interpretation of Nebuchadnezzar's dream, we see that there was a great statue that represented the kings of the kingdom of men. The head of gold was the Babylonian empire, which was then, the super power. The chest and arms of silver represented by the Medo-Persia Empire were slated to be the next super power that would succeed the king of Babylon. The belly and the thighs (hips) of brass, represented by the Greek empire would in turn succeed the Medo-Persia kingdom, followed by the legs of iron, represented by the Rome Empire. It was during this kingdom that the Lord was going to come and establish his kingdom. During the time of Jesus Christ, we see the Romans ruling over the children of Israel. And we have John the Baptist preaching repentance for the kingdom of God that was at hand. This is also confirmed by Jesus Christ introducing his kingdom and also asking repentenance, for the kingdom of God was at hand, meaning here. This is where God introduced, trained and taught about his kingdom (Mathew 5:1-48, Luke 17:21, KJV, etc). The final kingdom, represented by the European kingdom is mixed with iron and clay and would be divided into ten kingdoms. Each kingdom would succeed each other until the last kingdom is established and would be responsible for uniting or incorporating all kingdoms. Democracy will be the last standing government that will inspire all other governments to join them under the banner of a new world order. Under this democratic government or leadership influenced by Satan, they will wage war with God in attempt to prevent the second coming of God.

THE KINGDOM OF SATAN

> And Jesus knew their thoughts, and said unto them, "Every kingdom divided against itself is brought to desolation; and every city or house divided against itself shall not stand: And if Satan cast out Satan, he is divided against himself; how shall then his kingdom stand?"
>
> Matthew 12:25-26 (KJV)

THE COUNTERFEIT KINGDOM

Based on the above reference, Satan has a kingdom. His kingdom is well organized; however, it is built on darkness. This darkness stems from ignorance; that's how it thrives, by blinding the hearts and minds of its followers or believers. In order to fully understand this kingdom, we have to look at the character of its leader. Who is the leader of this kingdom? You guessed it— Satan, a fallen angel who desired God's position and sought to replace God. Due to his lack of creativity, inexperience, vision and leadership, he is not fit to be God or even to be considered as God. He is only an angel, a fallen one at that, and that is all he will ever be. It's only in the realm of the kingdom of men that he is considered to be a god. And this is only because he has managed to deceive mankind into thinking that he is a god. Scripture states, "He transforms himself as an angel of light" (2 Corinthians 11:14, KJV). Therefore, when he and his angels were expelled from heaven, they immediately plotted to hijack the kingdom given to mankind. Satan first sought to do this by tricking Eve, man's weaker vessel. This deception caused mankind (Adam) to forfeit his kingdom to Satan and he and his demons sought asylum or shelter within the human realm. They were now fugitives, wanted by God for escaping exile. Satan and his demons' influence over men slowly constructed a counterfeit kingdom that would run in conflict with God's kingdom; thus, Satan became the god of this world.

> In whom the god of this world hath blinded the minds of them which believe not, lest the light of the glorious gospel of Christ, who is the image of God, should shine unto them.
>
> 2 Corinthians 4:4 (KJV)

This Satanic kingdom will run in opposition to God's kingdom; meaning that whatever is not tolerated in God's kingdom, will be accepted in Satan's kingdom. In the kingdom of God, there is no murder, stealing, drunkenness, envy, adultery, fornication, sedition, witchcraft, lies, etc. All of these acts are part of Satan's kingdom. Let us examine what the Bible has to say about Satan's character. Doing so will provide a clearer understanding of why his kingdom operates the way it does. Let me first highlight the importance of one's character. Character is the good or bad behavior or the fruits of a person that influences self, people, household, ministry, community, society, government, or nation. Your fruits or behavior is determined by what character or tree you are made of; a bad character cannot bear good fruits (knowledge or behavior), and a good character cannot bear bad fruits (knowledge or behavior). In essence, every person is known by their behavior of fruits and it is through these fruits that one establishes or builds a family (household), ministry, corporation, company, businesses, government, or kingdom. Everyone is supposed to build a godly or good character; if we fail, God will destroy us. This is one of the reasons God, the Creator of heaven and earth, will destroy Satan's kingdom, once and for all, because its fruit (knowledge or behavior) is bad, i.e., fruits of the flesh (Galatians 5:19-21, KJV). For example, when a leader of a household is bad or wicked, his seeds or those within his household will necessarily be wicked or bad because they are taught and trained by him. They don't only inherit his wicked ways; but they do practice them; thus, you have the concept that a bad tree cannot bear good fruits. This is true of a pastor, minister, a government, nation, etc.; that is why the scripture says when the wicked are in authority, the people groan (Proverbs 29:2, KJV). This is why I encourage believers to examine the fruits of those that lead them; because your eternal salvation might be hinged upon those you follow, as scriptures confirm that if the blind lead the blind, both shall fall into a ditch. The first and second characteristic we see of the leader of this kingdom is that he is a murderer and a liar.

> Ye are of your father the devil, and the lusts of your father ye will do. He was a murderer from the beginning, and abode not in the truth, because there is no truth in him. When he speaketh a lie, he speaketh of his own: for he is a liar, and the father of it.
>
> John 8:44 (KJV)

The third and fourth characteristic we see is that he is a thief and a destroyer.

> The thief cometh not, but for to steal, and to kill, and to destroy: I am come that they might have life, and that they might have it more abundantly.
>
> John 10:10 (KJV)

No wonder the kingdom of men is filled with lies, murderer, greed, thieves, adultery, drunkenness, etc., because of the leader of this world. The god of this world is murdering, stealing, and destroying all those who are not protected by God, and those that do not accept Jesus Christ as Lord and Savior. This is the very reason why in the kingdom of Satan, the wicked, greedy, prideful, liars, etc., seem to advance and are rewarded in this kingdom; because the fact is that Satan prospers those who do his will. As the world progresses, unrighteousness becomes the norm, while righteousness is becoming a thing of the past; no longer is a man's word his bond. This is why the Bible cautions us Christians to come out from among them, for friendship with the world or Satan's kingdom is enmity with God.

This kingdom is not only fake or counterfeit but it is inferior and subject to God's kingdom, yet it is superior to the kingdom of men. However, this kingdom lacks creativity. For example, the so-called king of this kingdom cannot create; therefore, he is not a creator. He also lacks vision because he offers no hope or true freedom to those who ignorantly and blindly follow him. The only hope he offers them is eternal destruction because God, through Jesus Christ, will judge everyone. Therefore, ignorance is the blindness that derives from one's lack of salvation and decision to follow someone other than Jesus Christ due to their inability to understand God's vision, insight, or word. In fact, the only hope for this kingdom and those who blindly and ignorantly follow Satan and his demons is eternal damnation. This kingdom lacks uniqueness; therefore, everything the kingdom of God stands for is imitated and distorted in a contrary way by Satan's kingdom.

Satan is the king of this kingdom and he and his angels are on the run because they are fugitives and know that their time is short. Satan lacks a true throne; in fact, his throne is shared with the kingdom of men. Certainly, his throne cannot be in heaven because that is where God's throne is. And we know that in the beginning, God only created the heavens and the earth. So the only place left for the throne is here on earth among men; this is why he was so desperate to steal mankind's dominion.

> I know that you live in the city where Satan has his throne, yet you have remained loyal to me. You refused to deny me even when Antipas, my faithful witness, was martyred among you there in Satan's city.
>
> Revelation 2:13 (KJV)

Therefore, he must be sharing his throne with the kingdom of men. What do I mean by share his throne? I'm glad you ask. When I say he shares the throne with the kingdom of men, I mean he is the spiritual entity that influences the kingdom of men or government. And he normally possesses these kings or leaders, fills them with his pride, and makes them believe they are gods; then once he possesses them, he imposes his will on them, thereby making that country or nation a Satanic kingdom. These kings or leaders allow it because it verifies their power and control over their respective kingdom. Through this, they sell their soul to the devil, knowingly or unknowingly. Here is an example of a biblical record of a king who was not only influenced by Satan but was possessed with his spirit. Satan was the spiritual entity that governed the king of Tyrus.

> Moreover the word of the LORD came unto me, saying, Son of man, take up a lamentation upon the king of Tyrus, and say unto him, Thus saith the Lord GOD; Thou sealest up the sum, full of wisdom, and perfect in beauty. Thou hast been in Eden the garden of God; every precious stone was thy covering, the sardius, topaz, and the diamond, the beryl, the onyx, and the jasper, the sapphire, the emerald, and the carbuncle, and gold: the workmanship of thy tabrets and of thy pipes was prepared in thee in the day that thou wast created. Thou art the anointed cherub that covereth; and I have set thee so: thou wast upon the holy mountain of God; thou hast walked up and down in the midst of the stones of fire. 5Thou wast perfect in thy ways from the day that thou wast created, till iniquity was found in thee. By the multitude of thy merchandise they have filled the midst of thee with violence, and thou hast sinned: therefore, I will cast thee as profane out of the mountain of God: and I will destroy thee, O covering cherub, from the midst of the stones of fire. Thine heart was lifted up because of thy beauty, thou hast corrupted thy wisdom by reason of thy

> brightness: I will cast thee to the ground, I will lay thee before kings, that they may behold thee. Thou hast defiled thy sanctuaries by the multitude of thine iniquities, by the iniquity of thy traffick; therefore, will I bring forth a fire from the midst of thee, it shall devour thee, and I will bring thee to ashes upon the earth in the sight of all them that behold thee.
>
> Ezekiel 28:11-18, KJV

Once Satan seizes or influences a king, he automatically controls that kingdom. He and his demons will seek to expand that kingdom by waging war against other kingdoms, no matter the cause. Whether it be for oil, gold, diamonds, spices, free labor, politics, economics, religion, etc., war is waged to provide Satan's demons their own kingdom and their own influence. This cycle will repeat until the whole world is under his influence through kings and queens. The alliance of kings will be the determining factor of who is for them and who is against them and who they should destroy. Satan's government will control, manipulate, destroy, and overthrow through imperialism all government that is not a part of their alliance. Those kingdoms loyal to him will always do his bidding, even if there is no eminent threat or consensus within the alliance. In return, he gives them all the spoil of the land as a reward for their obedience. Other than Satan stealing the dominion given to Adam, he goes around parading the spoil of the world to anyone who will obey and worship him. We see that he tried to offer the spoil of the world to Jesus Christ in Matthew 4:8-10 (KJV). Scripture cautions us about the spoil of the world from Satan and tells us to not to give in to these deceptive tactics by selling our soul because we want power or riches.

> For what is a man profited, if he shall gain the whole world, and lose his own soul? Or what shall a man give in exchange for his soul?
>
> Matthew 16:26 (KJV)

THE KINGDOM OF MEN

DEMOCRACY, THE LAST GOVERNMENT

The kingdom of men is a kingdom where there is division of lands, states, countries, and nations. In each division, you have a ruler or a king over that territory or domain. It is not like the kingdom of God where there is no division of land or territory because there is only one king of all of heaven unlike the kingdom of men where there are many kings throughout the world. Therefore, it is not a fully integrated kingdom; it is a government where a king or ruler rules over a state, land, country, or nation. However, since Satan is the god of this fallen world, he seeks to integrate all the kings and their kingdoms into a one-world government or kingdom by uniting or merging all kingdoms into a global system through the spread of democracy, in hope of establishing a new world order. This will be the last standing government that will unify all world powers into a democratic government making up a global government. This new world order gives him total control over all humans, making him ruler over all of earth. He will control or influence all these earthly kings, including the Jews because they have rejected Jesus Christ, the true king of the world. Therefore, he will unite the world and build a world army that will seek to fight a war against God, Jesus Christ, and his army at his second coming. Any earthly government that has not embraced the rulership of God is indirectly or directly ruled or influence by the kingdom of Satan, the spiritual entity that hovers over the kings of men. As long as there is more than one king (president) and kingdom here on earth, there will always be wars and rumors of war because of man's cravings and desires to become the most powerful nation or government within it generation. This is why the concept or ideology of government will always breed wars or rumor of wars because kings feel the need to expand their territory or domain for resources and power and will do whatever it takes. This concept and ideology will always breed *imperialism*, when a stronger country dominates and controls a weaker country's resources. Under Satanic influences or control, he will allow such hostile takeover for those kings that comply with his demand, since he is the god of this world. In return, the kings will honor him provide sacrifices unto him or implement policies that promotes and contradict God's laws, while honoring Satan directly or indirectly violating God's commandment. This concept is what the kingdom of Satan implores over the kingdom of men. In order for the kingdom of men to be shielded and be protected from Satan's deception, they must accept and embrace the kingdom of God by accepting Jesus Christ as Lord and Savior. God's commandments are universal; everyone is accountable to uphold his universal law, the Ten Commandments.

TYPES OF GOVERNMENTS

Many governments have stood from the dawn of civilization to the awakening of modern civilization. Governments are the rule of order. Since the beginning of creation, mankind has sought out a government that will alienate God, the Creator of heaven and earth, from his creation. Biblical account has given insight to the rise and fall of these governments, thus attesting to the fact that no earthly government lasts forever. A modern definition of *government* is the governing authority (body of people or individual) within a political society, that is able to make laws, adjudicate disputes (policing or judges), and issue administrative decisions.

In Scripture, we see clearly that kings, queens or pharaohs were often the rulers or leaders of these governments. The type of governments instituted varied from government to government, region to region, or nation to nation, based on economic systems, political systems, or religious systems. However, the underlying objective of all government is primarily to protect its people from invaders and wars and to ensure peace and order by instituting and maintaining justice.

Most governments start out with innocent, benevolent intentions toward their citizens whom they have sworn to govern, whether by election, rights, royalty, or force; they have the powers to uphold law, enforce laws, or evade them. All earthly government has opposed or has begun to oppose the kingdom of God, through the subtle influence of Satan. Because it seeks to strip or alienate God from its laws and its presence and tries to destroy all that is God's.

> Why do the heathen rage, and the people imagine a vain thing? The kings of the earth set themselves, and the rulers take counsel together, against the Lord, and against his anointed, saying, "Let us break their bands asunder, and cast away their cords from us."
>
> Psalms 2: 1-3 (KJV)

Governments vary in leadership, region, and culture. Throughout human history, there have been at least ten to fifteen types of governments that have risen and fallen and some still stand only as historical monuments, as reminders of the power they once possessed, like the Egyptians, Babylonians, Romans, etc. The following are brief definitions of the different types of government that once existed or still exist:

Capitalist government is a government by which the citizens own their own business and property and must buy services, for example, healthcare, for private use.

Socialist government owns many of the larger industries and provides education, health, and welfare services while allowing citizens some economic choices.

Communist government owns all businesses and farms and provides its people healthcare, education, and welfare.

Dictatorship government consists of a single ruler with military control that forces its rule upon its people with no regard to opinion or individual rights.

Totalitarian government is a government where the citizens are forced to do the will of the government and are not permitted to leave the country.

Theocratic government is a form of government in which the God or a god or deities influence the governments of men through a set of religious beliefs.

Monarchy government has a king or queen with absolute power over a state, and his/her power is passed through the family line.

Plutocracy or Oligarchy government is a government ruled by an elite group, often the wealthy, who only favor their interests.

Democratic government is a political orientation of those who favor government by the people or by their elected representative. A democratic government allows the people or citizens to select a president (a king) through an election process, or votes, to govern them.

Biblical records of government fall within one or more of these brief descriptions above, with the exception of a democratic government. This is a new and improved government, carefully crafted, instituted, and influenced by Satan and is the sum total of all earthly governments. We will discover through the pages of this book that democracy is the hallmark of the institution or establishment of satanic government. He tried to implement this same system in heaven and it cost him his position in heaven; he and those that joined his rebellion were cast out of heaven. He desires to be God and has managed to deceive mankind into thinking that he is God. Based on this trickery, he is called the god of this world because he has mankind worshiping him as god. He needed a kingdom or territory by which he can rule and be worshiped as god. So for a long time he has been cast a shadow over mankind and has manipulated all earthly governments. And in these last days, he has instituted a new and improved form of government by taking power away from royal families where kingship is for a life time and is pass on to next of kin. And giving that power to the people to choose among themselves who should rule by his spirit with a restricted term limits government. Thus, democracy is putting power in the hands of the people and through the process of election, the people or the majorities select a representative or their king. Again, we know the majority is ignorant, and this is the tactics of the devil; he keeps those who follow him ignorant and blind and exploits them for his gain (2 Corinthians 4:3-4, KJV). You ask what Satan can possibly gain from us. For example, through Adam and Eve's deception or ignorance, he managed to usurp the dominion given to Adam and become our master. Our suffering since the beginning of time is not at the hands of God but at the hands of a wicked master, a fallen angel, whose plan is to destroy all those who bear the image of God because God threw them out of heaven. Democracy will become the primary mode by which mankind, under the influence of Satan, will seek to convert all government into democracy thus making earth the kingdom of Satan through the progressive process of uniting all earthly governments under one government for the primary purpose of one-world government, or kingdom. Democratic governments will lead and subdue all other government; those who will not convert to a democratic system will be destroyed until all of earth is under the authority of Satan. Democracy will be the last standing government that will gather all the army of the world to fight against God. Here is a brief contrast between the kingdom of God and the kingdom of men (democratic system). In the kingdom of God, God is the one that chooses you (John 6:44, KJV). In the kingdom of men (Democratic system), it is the people that choose a king. In the kingdom of God, all power is in the hands of the king (Matthew 28:18, KJV). In the kingdom of men (Democratic system), power is in the hands of the people or majority. In the kingdom of God, it is the king's will that is fulfilled.

> Thy kingdom come, Thy will be done in earth, as it is in heaven.
>
> Matthew 6:10 (KJV)

In the kingdom of men (democratic system), it is the will of the people that is fulfilled. In the kingdom of God, it is the king that dies for his people. In the kingdom of men (democracy) it is the people that die for the king. This parallels the conflict between the kingdom of God and the kingdom of men (democratic system), and the conflict is instigated by the devil and his demons. Again, *government* is defined as the governing authority (body of people or individual) within a political society, having authority to make laws, adjudicate disputes (policing or judges), and issue administrative decisions. However, I tend to define *government* as the administrative organization of mankind through a leader or a group. Thus, as we comb through the scriptures, we see similar references. The beginning or establishment of government was initiated when mankind was united by one language towards one common goal. Mankind had desire to build a tower whose height would reach the heavens. This desire was an attempt to create a government that would alienate or exclude God and to progressively move toward establishing a kingdom independent of God. So when God noticed their intentions, He came down from heaven and divided their language and scattered them throughout the face of the earth.

> And the whole earth was of one language, and of one speech. And it came to pass, as they journeyed from the east, that they found a plain in the land of Shinar; and they dwelt there. And they said one to another, go to, let us make brick, and burn them thoroughly. And they had brick for stone, and slime had they for morter. And

they said, go to, let us build us a city and a tower, whose top may reach unto heaven; and let us make us a name, lest we be scattered abroad upon the face of the whole earth. And the LORD came down to see the city and the tower, which the children of men builded. And the LORD said, Behold, the people is one, and they have all one language; and this they begin to do: and now nothing will be restrained from them, which they have imagined to do. Go to, let us go down, and there confound their language, that they may not understand one another's speech. So, the LORD scattered them abroad from thence upon the face of all the earth: and they left off to build the city. Therefore, is the name of it called Babel; because the LORD did there confound the language of all the earth: and from thence did the LORD scatter them abroad upon the face of all the earth.

Genesis 11:1-9 (KJV)

Therefore, with the same unity and common goal they had before they were scattered, those who understood each other or with the same language began to organize and dwell together based on their languages and cultures and sought ways to protect themselves internally and externally by making laws, which explains how tribes or governments were born. They could now trade, make laws, and adjudicate disputes based on their commonalities.

BEFORE THE ORGANIZATION (GOVERNMENT) OF MANKIND

Let me share with you what their world was like before the desire to build a tower or any thoughts of unity or the concept of organization. It was a world of anarchy, a state of lawlessness, a system with no government, where everyone did what was right in their own eyes. This world was heavily influenced by the fallen angels (demons), to the point that godly men who walk in the way of God were engaging in practices forbidden by God, like intermarrying and unequally yoking themselves. Unrighteousness became the norm, the way of life, and doing what was right was considered abnormal. The influx and influence of demonic activities show the intentions of these fallen angels—to infiltrate this physical world; and to express through human agents their perversions and destructive ways and, most of all, to make a statement to God that whatever good intention he had for the human race, they would steal, kill, or destroy. Yet God held man accountable for the wickedness that was upon the earth and brought judgment upon the human race by destroying all of mankind, because he gave earth to mankind.

> And it came to pass, when men began to multiply on the face of the earth, and daughters were born unto them, that the sons of God saw the daughters of men that they were fair; and they took them wives of all which they chose. And the Lord said, "My spirit shall not always strive with man, for that he also is flesh: yet his days shall be an hundred and twenty years. There were giants in the earth in those days; and also after that, when the sons of God came in unto the daughters of men, and they bare children

to them, the same became mighty men which were of old, men of renown. And God saw that the wickedness of man was great in the earth, and that every imagination of the thoughts of his heart was only evil continually. And it repented the LORD that he had made man on the earth, and it grieved him at his heart. And the LORD said, I will destroy man whom I have created from the face of the earth; both man, and beast, and the creeping thing, and the fowls of the air; for it repenteth me that I have made them.

Genesis 6:1-7 (KJV)

And we know how the story goes. God flooded the earth and drowned all those who had the breath of life and that did not fear and respect him. Noah had found favor in God's sight; as a result, God spared Noah, and by Noah's favor, he was able to save his household. So by Noah's righteousness, he was able to save himself and his family from the flood of the world. He only saved eight souls: Noah, his wife, his three sons, and the three sons' wives. Noah feared God and was the only man that continued to walk in integrity by having faith in God; so God, through faith, protected him and preserved him to continue the human race despite the wickedness of that generation. So, after the flood, as mankind began to multiply, they began to organize, to setup a government that would alienate or exclude God which was the birth of Babel when mankind sought to find their own way for fear of being destroyed by God again.

EXILE: THE BANISHMENT OF SATAN

And there was war in heaven: Michael and his angels fought against the dragon; and the dragon fought and his angels, And prevailed not; neither was their place found any more in heaven. And the great dragon was cast out, that old serpent, called the Devil, and Satan, which deceiveth the whole world: he was cast out into the earth, and his angels were cast out with him.

Revelation 12:7-9, (KJV)

THE TALE OF A MAD ANGEL

The aforementioned scripture states that there was a war in heaven. Michael, the chief commander of God's army, fought against the dragon and his angel. The same scripture lets us know who this dragon is: the old serpent called the Devil or Satan, which deceived the whole world. What happened? What led to this war in heaven? Was Lucifer, who is now Satan, not loved? What would cause a son to rebel against his father or creator? What were the reasons for this war? As I ponder these questions, my body quivers and I shake to my bones as I try to make sense of these thoughts. Lucifer, who was once the anointed angel, who used to lead worship in heaven, had thoughts of being God and from there on everything went wrong. This is one of the reasons the Bible cautions us to cast down every negative thought that seeks to exalt itself against the Word of God.

> Casting down imaginations and every high thing that exalted itself against the knowledge of God, and bringing into captivity every thought to the obedience of Christ.
>
> 2 Corinthians 10:5 (KJV)

It's through negative thoughts that people commit suicide, murder, adultery, and go against God's Word, etc. Because it is out of our thoughts that we make choices; then our choices will lead to our behavior or actions and our actions will lead to our destiny or fate. The audacity of Lucifer to desire something he couldn't have or be! This is not a position that could be filled by any created being, nor was it vacant for him to desire it. Besides, God said that he would not share his glory with anyone or anything, nor would his praise be given to a graven image (Isaiah 42:8, KJV). We just learned that the first criteria of being God is that you must be uncreated and be able to create; this alone disqualifies him; not to mention that he is not fit or equipped to be God or the creator of the universe. If he was to become a god, I would certainly not follow him or worship him because he does not have my best interests at heart and I know his only plan for our lives is to steal, kill, and destroy us for being created in the image and likeness of God. He dislikes God because God is great. Therefore, he continuously persecutes those who have confessed Jesus as Lord and savior. How do I know that? Because anyone who works against God or opposes his righteousness is an enemy of God. Jesus Christ himself said they will hate you because they hated him (Matthew 10:22, KJV). Therefore, he will try to destroy anything or anyone that resembles or reminds him of God, since he can't defeat God. Therefore, the next best thing to do is to go after his children. God is the one that has our best interests at heart, like he told the prophet Jeremiah:

> "For I know the thoughts that I think toward you," saith the Lord, "thoughts of peace, and not of evil, to give you an expected end."
>
> Jeremiah 29:11 (KJV)

These desires of wanting to be God puffed him up and made Lucifer a mad angel, because it's straight-up madness to try or even dare to think that a created being could be God. Caution, whenever you have someone thinking they are god or desiring to be a god, they are often under the influence of Satan because it is his desire to be God. Mankind has never desired to be God because they were created in the image and likeness of God. It is Satan who desires to be God in heaven; therefore, he goes around selling that fantasy or dream to mankind, causing the wrath of God to fall upon all those to try to compromise his integrity, the sacred title or position that only belongs to him and to him alone. God does not share his glory or position with anyone; only he alone is and should be called God, the Creator of all things. For example, it was Satan who introduced the concept of being gods to Eve and Adam in the garden. This great deception by Satan occurred when he told the first human beings on earth in the garden, particularly Eve, that if she ate of the forbidden fruit, the tree of knowledge consisting of good and evil; she would be like god, knowing good and evil.

> And the serpent said unto the woman, Ye shall not surely die: For God doth know that in the day ye eat thereof, then your eyes shall be opened, and ye shall be as gods, knowing good and evil.
>
> Genesis 3:4-5 (KJV)

Now the deception is that he did not reveal his true identity; therefore, he deceived Eve into thinking he was just a talking serpent and not really an ancient enemy of God. Also, when does knowing good and evil constitute being a god? Knowing good and evil does not make you God or gods; it's a lie from Satan. This is why Eve responded to God her maker that she was tricked or deceived by Satan. How did the devil trick or deceive her? Because, for one, she realized that the serpent was really Satan, the fallen angel; an adversary of God and two, knowing good and evil does not make you God. This is how she felt she had been tricked.

> And the Lord God said unto the woman, "What is this that thou hast done?" And the woman said, "The serpent beguiled me, and I did eat."
>
> Genesis 3:13 (KJV)

GOD'S IDENTITY HAS BEEN COMPROMISED (IDENTITY THEFT)

As a result of trying to covet God's position, we have the identity of God being compromised by Satan and his angels; through ignorance and deceptions, humans accept and make anything and anyone god.

> Not unto us, O Lord, not unto us, but unto thy name give glory, for thy mercy, and for thy truth's sake. Wherefore should the heathen say, "Where is now their God?" But our God is in the heavens: he hath done whatsoever he hath pleased. Their idols are silver and gold, the work of men's hands. They have mouths, but they speak not: eyes have they, but they see not. They have ears, but they hear not: noses have they, but they smell not: They have hands, but they handle not: feet have they, but they walk not: neither speak they through their throat. They that make them are like unto them; so is everyone that trusteth in them. O Israel, trust thou in the LORD: he is their help and their shield.

~10~O house of Aaron, trust in the LORD: he is their help and their shield. Ye that fear the LORD, trust in the LORD: he is their help and their shield.

Psalm 115-1-9 (KJV)

This is how many people are being misled or led astray by fallen angels (demons) disguising themselves as angles of lights or as God bringing about headache, heartache, false hopes and false healing to people who are desperately seeking God for peace. They are profaning the name of God through the art of identity theft and the sad thing about it is they have managed to train humans to become agents of deception to perpetuate a false image of God. This is what I call an identity theft because the title which only belongs to God is being compromised and is falsely used. As a result, God is falsely accused of all the evil things that happen in this world. This title or office of God should not be tampered with, played with, or taken lightly because it has holy attributes that uniquely and distinctly identify God as the Creator of heaven and earth. Due to the lack of respect and through ignorance, Satan has managed to taint this sacred title which only belongs to God by abusing and discrediting it; as a result, we have foolish human beings questioning the sovereignty of God by saying, if God is good, "Why do bad things happen to good people? Why are there so many evils in the world? Why did God let my mother, father, siblings die? Why did God let my father go on drugs or my mother to become a prostitute?" And all of this is not God's doing; it is Satan and his demons falsifying God's good name. Like we often say in church, "God is good all the time, and all the time, God is good." God, however, promised to destroy all those who misuse and take his name in vain and those who call themselves gods and are not God. He will utterly and miserably destroy them. As a result, we have many good people being misled into worshiping Satan and his demons because they are under the illusion that Satan is god the Creator or the grand architecture of the world. For example many occultists and those who practice witchcraft, voodoo, new age, freemasonry, etc are under the deception that Satan is god and they know no other power because he has blinded them so that they do not to know the truth. Therefore, they ignorantly worship him as god by praying to him, coveting worship that only belongs to God the creator of heaven and earth. This act of deception alone brings the wrath of God upon those who ignorantly worship Satan and his demons because it violates the first and second commandments.

> Thou shalt have no other gods before me. Thou shalt not make unto thee any graven image, or any likeness of anything that is in heaven above, or that is in the earth beneath, or that is in the water under the earth. Thou shalt not bow down thyself to them, nor serve them: for I the LORD thy God am a jealous God, visiting the iniquity of the fathers upon the children unto the third and fourth generation of them that hate me;
>
> Exodus 20: 3-5 (KJV)

This is one of many ways that Satan indirectly destroys us by causing us to violate God's laws or commands, thereby bringing upon us the judgment or the wrath of God on us. Satan wants our worship; therefore he stops at nothing and would do whatever is within his limits to cause us, the human race to worship him, by reason of coveting worship that only belongs to God through the process of identity theft.

> And he causeth all, both small and great, rich and poor, free and bond, to receive a mark in their right hand, or in their foreheads: And that no man might buy or sell, save he that had the mark, or the name of the beast, or the number of his name.
>
> Revelation 13: 16-17 (KJV)

None of the fallen angel's worship Satan because he is an angel. They are his peers, his equals. Angels do not worship other angels, just like human beings do not worship other human beings. Both humans and angels are made to worship God and God alone. When humans or angels worship Satan, it is another prime example of Satan compromising or coveting something that does not belong to him and God, the Creator of heaven and earth, is not going to allow this for long. Jesus Christ even warned Satan, when he said to him he should worship the lord his God and him alone he should worship (Luke 4:8, KJV). However, through Satan's trickery and wisdom, uses his wisdom to fool all those who follow him both fallen angels and men. But some follow him based on what he has promised them, even though these fallen angels know it's a lost cause and humans who willingly submit to his leadership or influences are only in it for what they can get from him. But the good news is that Satan's wisdom is foolishness when it comes to God. Therefore he can fool fallen angels and men but he cannot fool God.

Just the thought alone of being God is a sin, and more, to desire the same is inconceivably abominable because to be God requires one to not only be able to create but also uncreate. The desire to covet something that is not yours is a grave sin, which the Lord constantly warned us about throughout the scriptures, particularly in the first of the Ten Commandments. This desire led to Satan premeditating over how to overthrow God. So, he began his conspiracy against God his Creator by trying to win the hearts of the angels in heaven. He went around to some of the angels and asked them to join him in revolting against God. He stated to the angels that he was getting ready to institute a new system that would restrict and limit God as King of heaven forever. This new system would put term limits on how long the King of heaven could rule. This new system would empower the angels by allowing them to hold elections and to vote into power who they want to be their king or god. Some of the angels reported this secret coup to God, even though God already knew

Democracy in Heaven

what was happening because he is all knowing. This was Satan's desire of leadership; thus, the concept of democracy or demon craft was born in heaven in the heart of Satan. It did not fly in heaven, but he knew it would work here on earth because mankind is fragile and ignorant of his wiles. He stated that he was going to lead this revolution against God in heaven in hope to become the second king or god in heaven. As a result of him going around asking the angels to help him set up a democratic system in heaven, he recruited at least one third of the angels in heaven. One third of God's angels in heaven had signed up and agreed to help him campaign against God or help him revolt against God. Now one third of the angels in heaven is a lot of angels. If we select the smallest number of angels that had signed up or agreed to help him, it would be at least over a million angels that joined Satan's rebellion against God. This train of thought, or concept or reasoning is evident if we ask ourselves how Satan convinced one third of God's sons or God's angels to join him in revolting or rebelling against God. We could safely answer that he schemes included actively recruiting for the new order he intended to start in heaven. This craftiness and cunning reminds me of Absalom, King David's third son, who also schemed against his father's throne. He was the most handsome guy in all of Israel (just like Lucifer), well favored and loved by the people. Lucifer, being a worship leader, must have also been well favored and loved by some of the angels.

> But in all Israel, there was none to be so much praised as Absalom for his beauty: from the sole of his foot even to the crown of his head there was no blemish in him. And when he polled his head (for it was at every year's end that he polled it: because the hair was heavy on him, therefore he polled it:), he weighed the hair of his head at two hundred shekels after the king's weight.
>
> 2 Samuel 14:25-26 (KJV)

Absalom usurped his father's throne through the craftiness of empathy. Absalom would rise up early in the morning and stand by the gates, greeting all who entered or exited. He would listen to the people's complaints before they saw the king, his father. He would offer his insight, hoping to diminish the king's authority, and tell them that if he was the king, he would personally judge all their matters. Eventually, he won the hearts of the people, his popularity grew, and he set up his own military coup to overthrow his father in an attempt to take over his father's kingdom so that he could be the next king of Israel.

> And it came to pass after this, that Absalom prepared him chariots and horses, and fifty men to run before him. And Absalom rose up early, and stood beside the way of the gate: and it was so, that when any man that had a controversy came to the king for judgment, then Absalom called unto him, and said, "Of what city art thou?" And he said, "Thy servant is of one of the tribes of Israel. And Absalom said unto him, See, thy matters are good and right; but there is no man deputed of the king to hear thee. Absalom said moreover, oh that I were made judge in the land, that every man which hath any suit or cause might come unto me, and I would do him justice! And it was so, that when any man came nigh to him to do him obeisance, he put forth his hand, and took him, and kissed him. And in this manner, did Absalom to all Israel that came to the king for judgment: so Absalom stole the hearts of the men of Israel. And it came to pass after forty years, that Absalom said unto the king, I pray thee, let me go and pay my vow, which I have vowed unto the LORD, in Hebron. For thy servant vowed a vow while I abode at Geshur in Syria, saying, If the LORD shall bring me again indeed to Jerusalem, then I will serve the LORD. And the king said unto him, Go in peace. So, he arose, and went to Hebron. But Absalom sent spies throughout

> all the tribes of Israel, saying, as soon as ye hear the sound of the trumpet, then ye shall say, Absalom reigneth in Hebron. And with Absalom went two hundred men out of Jerusalem, that were called; and they went in their simplicity, and they knew not anything. And Absalom sent for Ahithophel the Gilonite, David's counselor, from his city, even from Giloh, while he offered sacrifices. And the conspiracy was strong; for the people increased continually with Absalom. And there came a messenger to David, saying, the hearts of the men of Israel are after Absalom. And David said unto all his servants that were with him at Jerusalem, Arise, and let us flee; for we shall not else escape from Absalom: make speed to depart, lest he overtake us suddenly, and bring evil upon us, and smite the city with the edge of the sword.
>
> 2 Samuel 15:1-14 (KJV)

Scriptures caution us to be as "wise as a serpent and harmless as a dove" (Matthew 10:16), because the wisdom and craftiness of Satan is astounding yet admonishable. So, God dealt a swift, ecclesiastical censorship by excommunicating him to preserve more than the two thirds of the angels that did not join his rebellion or coup against God, even though we know that not even all of the angels in heaven combined together could overthrow God or could equate to his power, for we know that he is all powerful.

And who knows, if God did not put a stop to his masquerade, maybe one half of the angels would have joined this revolt. Like I said, it would not have made a difference because God is all powerful. We see a replica of the old serpent's tactic being perpetuated on mankind during the tribulation to the point that God has to shorten time or else no flesh will be saved, possibly even the very elect.

> And except those days should be shortened, there should no flesh be saved: but for the elect's sake those days shall

be shortened. Then if any man shall say unto you, Lo, here is Christ, or there; believe it not.

> Matthew 24:22-24 (KJV)

The thought of Satan trying to overthrow God really, really frightens me. I imagine God on his throne, exuberating in the worship of the angels, and Lucifer leading the worship. Then suddenly, there were a great commotion; Lucifer and his angels executed their plan of attack on my Father God on his throne to try to overthrow or execute God. This was no surprise to God because he is all knowing (omniscient); he knows what is in the heart of men and angels before they even act on it. That's why he had his chief commander of his army in place to intercept Satan and his angels' attack. This thought is really painful and it brings tears to my eyes because of my love for God our Father, who art in heaven. I'm not saying that Father God is weak or helpless or old because we know that he is all powerful (omnipotent), but just imagine the lack of appreciation of all the love and benevolence Father God gives to everyone and his continual mercifulness, for we know that God is love, says scripture. This monstrous act of uncontrolled lustfulness, of covetousness, selfishness, and against father God by one of his created creatures shows Satan's short sightedness because he started something that he could not finish. I'm glad that God commander in Chief Michael the archangel to disarm Lucifer and his angels and expelled them out of heaven and exiled them to earth to await God's impending judgment upon them.

> And there was war in heaven: Michael and his angels fought against the dragon; and the dragon fought and his angels, and prevailed not; neither was their place found any more in heaven." And the great dragon was cast out, that old serpent, called the Devil, and Satan, which deceiveth the whole world: he was cast out into the earth, and his angels were cast out with him.
>
> Revelation 12:7-9 (KJV)

EXILED TO EARTH

The book of Isaiah gives us insight into Lucifer's desires. It was pride that led to his fall from heaven by reason of starting a revolution in heaven to try to oust God, the King of kings and his continual desire to want to be God, even after he and his angels were outcast or evicted out of heaven and exiled to earth.

> How art thou fallen from heaven, O Lucifer, son of the morning! How art thou cut down to the ground, which didst weaken the nations! For thou hast said in thine heart, I will ascend into heaven, I will exalt my throne above the stars of God: I will sit also upon the mount of the congregation, in the sides of the north: I will ascend above the heights of the clouds; I will be like the most high. Yet thou shalt be brought down to hell, to the sides of the pit.
>
> Isaiah 14:12-15 (KJV)

This is the reason I believe Satan and his demons were cast out of heaven and exiled to earth. Pride was the strength of Satan's rebellion in heaven. What is pride? *Pride, as defined by the dictionary, is a high or inordinate opinion of one's own dignity, importance, merit, or superiority, whether as cherished in the mind or as displayed in bearing, conduct, etc.*

> The highway of the upright is to depart from evil: he that keepeth his way preserveth his soul. Pride goeth before destruction, and an haughty spirit before a fall.
>
> Proverb 16:17-18 (KJV)

Satan, because of his rank and beauty, tried to exalt himself above the throne of God which was impossible. He thought he could be a better god than his maker. Satan and his demons miscalculated the power of God; they thought God was their peer or their equal. Father God knew everything that was going down, just like Jesus Christ knew, when he was here on earth; everything that was in the human heart, what mankind thought and believed before they even said it. In fact, he told his disciples to their faces plainly, he had chosen twelve of them, and one of them was a devil:

> Jesus answered them, "Have not I chosen you twelve, and one of you is a devil?"
>
> John 6:70 (KJV)

So, Father God knew when Satan was going around to the angels in heaven, conspiring against Him; making promises to the angels that he could not keep; promising all those who joined him that he would give them a higher position in his administration or kingdom. God knew of the false promises he was making to the angels; how else could Satan convinced one third of the angels to follow him? He must have promised them something unless these angles were not so smart and we know that is not the case. Angels are not stupid, or are they? Even though Lucifer was the most beautiful angel in heaven, I'm sure it was not because of his looks that the other angels joined his rebellion against God. We see this pattern all the time in our life and throughout scriptures, when Satan would cook up some false promises to manipulate us to forfeit our soul. He tried it with Jesus Christ, the Son of God during his earthly ministry when Jesus was led into the wilderness to be tempted by the devil. Did not Satan promise Jesus the kingdom of the world if he fell down and worshiped him?

> And the devil, taking him up into a high mountain, shewed unto him all the kingdoms of the world in a moment of time. And the devil said unto him, "All this power will I give thee, and the glory of them: for that is delivered unto me; and to whomsoever I will I give it. If thou therefore

> wilt worship me, all shall be thine." And Jesus answered and said unto him, get thee behind me, Satan: for it is written, thou shalt worship the Lord thy God, and him only shalt thou serve.
>
> Luke 4: 5-8 (KJV)

Once Jesus was victorious, he warned us of the enemy's scheme by saying that it does not profit us to gain the whole world and to lose our soul.

> For what is a man profited, if he shall gain the whole world, and lose his own soul? Or what shall a man give in exchange for his soul?
>
> Matthew 16:26 (KJV)

Because of Satan's empty promises, he caused one third of God's angels to lose their relationship with God, their positions, and most importantly, their souls. Oh yes, angels have souls, but the soul they have is not redeemable like the human soul; likewise, even animals have souls, but the soul animals have is not redeemable like yours and mine. Only the human soul is redeemable because God, through Jesus Christ, has forever atoned for our sins. Doesn't this make you feel special? This is how much God loves you. He came to die for you and me. So much that he himself said we are of more value than the birds of the air (Matthew 6:25-26).

When they were cast down to earth, they were trapped between time and space and were in utter darkness. When I say they were in utter darkness, I mean angels were created to dwell in the light of God. Anything apart from dwelling in God's presence would be total darkness. We got a glimpse of this truth when Moses climbed Mount Sinai to receive the Law, the Ten Commandments, for the second time; he was in God's presence for forty days and forty nights and we saw what happened to his face when he came down from the mountain. Being in God's presence for that long caused his face to shine, even to the point of disappearing because anything that dwells in the presence of God will begin to illuminate; Moses's molecular structure was fading. When he came down from the mountain from God's presence, he still had the glory of God shining on his face. When he went to speak to the children of Israel, at first they did not recognize him because of the brightness of his face. He had to convince them that it was him, Moses. His face was shining so much that they had to put a veil or a cover over his face until that brightness or glory faded away. The covering or the veil that was put on Moses's face had a spiritual connotation that is further explained in 2 Corinthians 3:7-18. Moses's illumination was a sign of his presence with God. For example, have you ever tried looking directly at the sun, especially when it's shining on you. What happens when you stare at it for a long period of time? What happens when you stop looking at it or turn away from looking at it? Doesn't it seem like you can't see anything at all, and doesn't it seem like you're blind? It is like your eyes have to refocus or adjust themselves. Another good example is when the Apostle Paul was on his way to Damascus. Let's read it:

> And Saul, yet breathing out threatenings and slaughter against the disciples of the Lord, went unto the high priest, And desired of him letters to Damascus to the synagogues, that if he found any of this way, whether they were men or women, he might bring them bound unto Jerusalem. And as he journeyed, he came near Damascus: and suddenly there shined round about him a light from heaven: And he fell to the earth, and heard a voice saying unto him, Saul, Saul, why persecutest thou me? And he said, Who art thou, Lord? And the Lord said, I am Jesus whom thou persecutest: it is hard for thee to kick against the pricks. And he trembling and astonished said, Lord, what wilt thou have me to do? And the Lord said unto him, Arise, and go into the city, and it shall be told thee

> what thou must do. And the men which journeyed with him stood speechless, hearing a voice, but seeing no man. And Saul arose from the earth; and when his eyes were opened, he saw no man: but they led him by the hand, and brought him into Damascus. And he was three days without sight, and neither did eat nor drink.
>
> Acts 9:1-9 (KJV)

What I'm saying is that angels were meant to be in the light of God or dwell in God's presence; and when they turn away or look away to try to find their own way, they thrust themselves into darkness, because anything apart from God is darkness. Likewise, are we who when the light of God comes into our heart and when we reject it or turn away, we position ourselves in darkness or become ignorant of God's light (true knowledge).

FUGITIVES

SATAN AND HIS DEMONS ESCAPE EXILE

> And the earth was without form, and void; and darkness was upon the face of the deep. And the Spirit of God moved upon the face of the waters.
>
> Genesis 1:2 (KJV)

This passage describes the condition of Satan and his demons after being cast out of heaven—utter darkness. They were trapped between time and space; they could not influence earth, because they are immaterial beings. The only way they can affect earth, the material world, is to possess a human being. They occupied the air; that's why Scripture says Satan is the prince of the air.

> Wherein in time past ye walked according to the course of this world, according to the prince of the power of the air, the spirit that now worketh in the children of disobedience: Among whom also we all had our conversation in times past in the lusts of our flesh, fulfilling the desires of the flesh and of the mind; and were by nature the children of wrath, even as others.
>
> Ephesians 2:2-3 (KJV)

They witnessed Adam and Eve's relationship with Father God, their creator. When Father God would arrive during the cool of the day and fellowship with Adam and Eve, they envied that fellowship, especially Satan. Satan and his demons were behind the scenes and jealously observed God provide Adam dominion over all earth to rule and subdue over everything or anything that is within the earth's realm. How else did Satan know that God had told them to not to eat from the tree of knowledge of good and evil, since he is not all knowing (Genesis 3:1, KJV)? This dominion over earth included Satan and his demon because he and his demons were cast down to earth before Adam was crowned or given dominion over all of earth. This dominion God gave to Adam included ruling over all of these fallen angels. The devil and his demons were very upset when they heard and witnessed God crowning Adam as king over all of earth and creating a queen, the king's companion, a suitable helpmate who will assist him in ruling all of earth. I believe that God intentionally did this because he wanted to show Satan and all those fallen angels, those who were foolish to follow Satan's scheme, who is the boss. Since they did not want to be ruled by him in heaven, maybe they would like to be ruled by inferior human beings. Therefore, God created lower, inferior creatures to rule over them by creating dirt creatures (humans) to rule over them. This reminds me of a phrase in the scripture that cautions that if we don't praise him, he will cause the rock to praise him (Luke 19:40, KJV). Since Satan and his fallen angels refused to continue to give God praise and worship in heaven, he made dirt creatures (humans) to praise and worship him; thus, we replaced them and filled the vacant position in heaven the fallen angels abandoned. Let us think about it; here you have one of the most beautiful, powerful angels, the anointed cherub who held one of the most powerful positions in heaven being made subject to human beings, a far weaker creature than he. For me, this is very humiliating and I know Satan's pride was eating him up because he is a prideful creature. It hints, from God's perspective, *You wanted to be Me, but you can't be Me, so I will make creatures from the dust of the ground (humans), the ground I walk on and give them authority over you and all those who were foolish to follow you and your scheme, for you or no one is My equal.* Instead of being exalted, he was abased to the lowest position ever—to be subjected to dirt people, humans. If this was not a direct slap to the face, I don't know what you would call it. This was a reality check for Satan and his demons that forced them to realize that there can only be one God, the God who creates and who gives authority to whomsoever he wants. This humiliation reminds me of King Nebuchadnezzar in the book of Daniel and how God stripped his kingdom away from him and drove him into the wilderness to be converted to an animal, eating grass, until he lifted his head and hands to God and acknowledged him as the only one and true God.

> The king spake, and said, "Is not this great Babylon, that I have built for the house of the kingdom by the might of my power, and for the honour of my majesty?" While the word was in the king's mouth, there fell a voice from heaven, saying, "O King Nebuchadnezzar, to thee it is spoken; The kingdom is departed from thee."
>
> Daniel 4:30-37 (KJV)

God knew what the outcome was going to be in the garden, that Satan, through his craftiness and corrupt wisdom, was going to entice through deception and deceive mankind to sin against him by causing them to indirectly join him and his demons in their rebellion against Him. This was all a part of God's plan before he even created heaven and earth and the garden to put man and his wife. Since he is all knowing, he had already made provisions to deal with all of Satan's tricks, direct or indirect attacks or plans to overthrow him. Satan and his demons can't go back to heaven because they have been kicked out and they were banished or exiled to earth. In essence, Satan and his demons were homeless and were desperately seeking an opportunity for a shelter within the human world. Satan, leader of the rebels, lacks vision; he could not even create light to lead his demons out of darkness, make a land or country of their own nor even build a shelter for those fallen angels that helped him to rebel against their maker. That's to show you that he is not a creator. God has given full authority to Adam, king over all of earth. Therefore, they were under the jurisdiction of Adam. Therefore, Adam or mankind had dominion over Satan and all the fallen angels. Since they did not want to be ruled by God, maybe they would listen to Adam. If Adam would have continued to exercise his authority over earth and creation, mankind as a whole would not be in this present condition, but thank God Jesus, through his obedience, rescued us from the wiles of the enemy. God specifically told Adam and gave him power and rights over everything in the earth: anything that sneezes, spits, breathes, crawls, walks, swims, flies, etc. So therefore, Adam was without an excuse because he should have used his power or authority to annihilate the serpent in self-defense; he should have dragged or pulled that serpent out of that tree and chopped him into pieces or stomped on him until his head was crushed. Okay, maybe that's too drastic and Adam should not resort to such violence, but at least he should have put the serpent in his place, rebuking him like Jesus did when he said, "Get thee behind me, Satan." Adam did not only fail God, but he failed his wife because he was supposed to protect her, and finally, he failed all of humanity. Adam's negligence or failure caused his posterity to bear the consequences of his sin, and the enemy, who are Satan and his rebels (demons), who have no problem exercising the dominion Adam forfeited to him. As a result, he does not even think twice or hesitate in destroying us; in fact, "He is walking around seeking whom he may devour or destroy" (1 peter 5:8, KJV). Since Adam did not exercise his authority to crush the head of the serpent, who is Satan, Scripture goes on to say that the second or last Adam, which is Jesus, will come and crush his head. Scripture says between the woman seed who is Jesus Christ and the seed of the serpent who will be the antichrist; the seed of the serpent (anti-Christ) will bruise Jesus's heel which we know represents a temporary wound which is the suffering that Jesus Christ went through to redeemed us from the curse of the law while here on earth. And the seed of the woman, which is Jesus, will bruise the serpent's head which is a sign of a fatal wound to Satan's head (Genesis 3:15, KJV). This is how you execute a serpent by stomping or cutting his head off.

The whole of earth is supposed to be under man's dominion and not under Satan and his demons' control. They knew the only way they could affect or impact this physical world was to gain entrance into the human world. Though they were cast to earth, they could not affect this world because they were not of the earth and did not possess human bodies; they are immaterial beings, or spiritual beings. The only way they could be effective here on this earth was to somehow influence Adam into sinning against God, thereby causing mankind to come away from God's protections and causing mankind to also be in rebellion with God. This rebellion caused Adam and Eve to be evicted out of the garden of Eden, to be exiled to earth where they were created and where Satan and his demons were in exile But the difference is the fallen angels are confined to time and space because they are spiritual beings, while mankind is confined to time and earth because they are material beings. So now earth is the temporary holding place or a jail cell for the fallen, whether it is angels or humans, until the Day of Judgment, the day of reckoning. Earth also became the uniting force of fallen angels and fallen humans, where Satan and his demons began to coach mankind in all kinds of witchcrafts. Earth became the jail cell that houses both fallen angels and fallen men as a result of their rebellion; mankind is now awaiting their sentences from God, who sits on the throne. There are some who are sentenced for life (human), who can have their sentence shortened once they plead guilty and accept God's redemptive plan by confessing Jesus Christ as Lord and Savior and those who refuse to plead guilty are simply on death row. There are those whose sentence is execution because of the severity of their crime: treason, conspiracy, pride, etc,; these are the fallen angels, whose punishment is hell with no possible chance of ever being free or paroled. They are just waiting to be executed and while they are waiting, they are causing chaos and trying to deceive humans by blinding them with darkness so that they will not receive or accept Jesus as Lord and Savior so that they could be pardoned. If they accept Jesus Christ, they will be immediately free from earth to enter back into God's society, and their citizenship in heaven will be reinstated. This is why scriptures explain to every believer of Jesus Christ that "...though we are in this world, we are not of this world," (John 17:14,16, KJV) because our real citizenship is in heaven. But those humans who are released and do not live a transformed life but conform to the world will again go back to incarceration, which is Egypt, which symbolizes slavery or bondage and will be certainly condemned to hell. And there are some humans who, while in jail (world or Egypt), committed additional crimes and are resentenced to death (hell).

Satan, through subtle deception, stripped Adam of his dominion as king of earth and coveted God's position as the god of men. This victorious act of deception was a defeat for mankind but a triumph for Satan and his demons. This act created an open door for Satan and his demons to escape exile by entering into the human realm or world. This open door was an indirect invitation from mankind that allowed Satan and his demons to seek shelter and to cohabitate with mankind. Their escape made them a fugitive on earth because fallen angels and human were not to interact with one another. As a result, they began to reshape our minds, our thinking, our behavior, our lifestyles, etc., from the ways of God. They completely restructured our way of living, erasing all righteous behaviors. As a result, it got so bad that God regretted that he made man and looked for and found a man on earth with whom he could make a covenant to save that man (Noah) and his family while he destroyed everything on earth that had the breath of life (Genesis 6:1-7, KJV).

THE TALE OF A MAD ANGEL

I can now imagine what Satan and his demons' conversation was like once they noticed that they were cast out of heaven and were now homeless. I can imagine the defeat, disgust, bruises, and the contemplation of what just happened—nowhere to go, nothing but darkness. Think with me; let's imagine when they were cast out of heaven into darkness, there was a great confusion here on earth in the spiritual realm. Some of the demons were sorrowful, regretful, and fearful, because they had lost the war in heaven and their relationship with God (Revelation. 12:7-9, KJV). They were more hurt because they had rejected God, their Maker, and could no longer dwell in God's presence. Some realized they made a big mistake and that this mistake was forever, because God does not forgive angels that sin (2 Peter 2:4, KJV). They learned a significant, eternal lesson not to follow Satan's schemes and to not desire something that is not theirs. Lucifer, the fallen angel and his wishful desires caused the life and eternal damnation of millions, if not, billions of angels. Besides, he has no military skills because he was a worship leader. The frustration the fallen angels felt was one of the saddest days in angelic history. They lost everything: their homes, their families, their companions, etc. I can now just imagine what was going on, what their conversations were like when they realized that they have been cast down to earth. Scripture goes on to confirm that Jesus saw them being cast down to earth like lightening.

> And he said unto them, I beheld Satan as lightning fall from heaven.
>
> Luke 10:18 (KJV)

Here is a behind-the-scene version I imagine their conversation was like as a result of their banishment:

Demons: *Now what?*

Satan: *What do you mean, "Now what"?*

Demons: *What are we going to do now? We can't go back because Michael and his angels are too strong for us; we can't beat them.*

Notes: Some of the demons said they were going back to ask for forgiveness by pleading with God because they had been tricked by Lucifer. Those fallen angels came to God and pleaded for mercy. God placed them in a holding place and till this present day, they are still in a reserved holding, awaiting God's judgment.

Notes: While in exile, they saw the loving relationship Adam and Eve had with God, their Maker. They saw God give Adam dominion over everything on earth. They were mad and they said to one another, *How he can make these inferior beings rule over us?* But God intentionally did that as a statement that he could create dirt creatures and make them rule over those fallen angels who seek his authority.

Demons: *Satan, did you hear that?*

Satan: *Hear what?*

Demons: *God just made this dust creature, Adam, king over us.*

Satan: *Yes, I can hear; I'm not deaf. Not for long; I will show these dirt creatures who is who.*

Demons: *Show them what? Who is who?*

Satan: *Yes, who is boss. If God thinks I'm going to let these spit, dirty people rule me, he has another think coming.*

Demons: *How are you going to do that?*

Satan: *Just watch; just watch.*

Demons: *Just watch what? I think Archangel Michael hit you too hard on your head.*

There was a great laughter among the demons.

Satan, not paying them any mind, fixed his eyes on Adam and Eve, observing and studying them carefully. He realized the weakness of Eve; for some reason, God would always communicate to Adam, and Adam would instruct his wife. This is consistent throughout Scripture. For example, God directly spoke with Abraham and Abraham would then let Sarah, his wife, know what God had told him. That's why, when the devil told Eve she would be like God, knowing good and evil, she fell for it; she wanted to stand with Adam in the presence of God. For some reason, that thought or notion penetrated throughout tradition, even to the point that when Mary was sitting at Jesus's feet, listening to all that Jesus was saying, her sister Martha came and asked Jesus to send her into the kitchen to help her because she couldn't do it alone.

> Now it came to pass, as they went, that he entered into a certain village: and a certain woman named Martha received him into her house. And she had a sister called Mary, which also sat at Jesus' feet, and heard his word. But Martha was cumbered about much serving, and came to him, and said, Lord, dost thou not care that my sister hath left me to serve alone? bid her therefore that she help me. And Jesus answered and said unto her, Martha, Martha, thou art careful and troubled about many things: But one thing is needful: and Mary hath chosen that good part, which shall not be taken away from her.
>
> Luke 10:38-42 (KJV)

Satan: *Look how innocent and naïve they are. No experience of kingship or rulership. I am going to talk to them as soon as God leave.*

Demons: *What are going to say to them?*

Satan: *Just watch.*

He studied Adam and Eve carefully, looking for an opportunity.

Note: Lucifer turned himself into a serpent and acted as one of the animals of the garden and slipped and slid down the forbidden tree, the tree of knowledge of good and evil.

Demons, among themselves: *What is Satan up to?*

Demon: *I know what he doing; he is going to cause them to disobey God's command and strip their authority from them, thereby opening a doorway for us to enter into their world or their body, and we will be able to influence and control them and do whatever we want with them. They will naïvely make us their gods. Once they disobey God's command, God will throw them out of the garden, like he did us, out of his presence in heaven. Thereby, they will not be under God's protection. We will then unite with them who are willing to obey us; those who are not, we will destroy.*

Satan finally got Eve's attention.

Satan: *Hey, Eve, did God say you should not eat of every tree in the garden?*

Eve: *Yes, we may eat of every fruit of the trees in the garden, but the fruit of the tree in the midst of the garden, God said we should not eat it or touch it, or else we will die.*

Satan: *Die? That's absurd; you won't die. How can you die from just eating a fruit unless it's poisonous or spoiled? Does it look rotten to you?*

Eve: *No.*

Satan: *Die? Give me a break. God knows the day you eat it, your eyes will be opened, and you will be as gods, knowing good and evil.*

Eve: *Well, well, I don't know. Let me go get my husband, because you're talking like you're in charge.*

Satan: *Who, Adam? Go ahead, go get him.*

Eve: *Yes, Adam, my husband, the one who is in charge of everything in this garden.*

Note: Eve came walking with Adam; Satan slightly hid himself as he observed them talking. Eve explained to Adam what the serpent had told her, saying the snake on the tree was trying to tell her that the forbidden fruits would make them wise and that Father God was hiding something from them, and that was why he did not want them to eat it.

Satan slipped out of his hiding.

Satan: *Hey, Adam, my man, I was just telling your reasonable wife that I don't see anything physically wrong with this fruit; in fact, I've been eating of this fruit, and I'm not dead. But*

Eve, your reasonable wife, said she can't even touch it or else will die, and look, I'm touching it.

Then Satan threw a fruit to Eve, and she caught it. He then said:

> Satan: *See, Eve, you're touching it. Did you die? In fact, all the fruits in the garden are good for food. God is a good God, and cannot create anything bad or poisonous that will be harmful for you or kill you. It would be against his nature. In fact, if the fruits on this tree are deadly, what is it doing is this beautiful garden? It should be cut down and thrown into the fire. Besides, I did not plant or create this tree or put it here.*

> And he insisted on the beauty of the fruits of the tree.

> Eve looked up and saw that the tree was good for food and that it was pleasant to the eyes and was a tree to be desired to make one wise. She took of the fruit and ate it and gave unto her husband, and he did eat.

Note: Scripture says that Eve ate first and nothing happened. It was when Adam ate that both of their eyes were opened because Adam had the dominion and not Eve. If Adam did not eat of the fruit, nothing would have happened. It was when he ate that death entered the human body, or the human world.

> Wherefore, as by one-man sin entered into the world, and death by sin; and so death passed upon all men, for that all have sinned:
>
> > Roman 5:12 (KJV)

So when Adam saw that nothing happened to Eve when she ate the forbidden fruit, he thought it was okay to eat instead of obeying God. So it was through Adam's disobedience, not by Eve's sin, that sin entered the world. Satan relentlessly desires to be God and will not accept an inferior dirt creature to rule over him.

He wanted Adam's crown, Adam's kingship, mankind's dominion. It was for this same reason he was expelled out of heaven; he tried the same thing in heaven by desiring to be God and wanting

God's position but was not successful and it cost him his position and he was evicted out of heaven.

Now that we have seen what happened in the garden, let us carefully analyze it by also looking at the spiritual aspect of what had happened in the garden, particularly concerning the tree of knowledge of good and evil. Understanding this spiritual truth, I believe, will truly bless us and it will begin to unlock some of the doubt we often have regarding the Scripture—doubt about how one person's sin can render all of humanity to die. Doubt about why God put the tree there if he knew Adam was going to sin. Also, reason would have me conclude that the fruit was poisonous. God created it; if everything that he created is good, what was it doing in the garden? Apprehension of this revelation concerning the fruit of the tree of knowledge of good and evil is the foundational or fundamental understanding of biblical maturity which starts the process of understanding and making sense of the Bible. It is like all the pieces of the puzzle are rightly coming together. To embark on this revelation concerning what really happened in the garden, we first have to see what Scripture or the Bible says about "fruits." First of all, let us consider what Jesus Christ told Satan, or the devil the same serpent that caused Adam and Eve to sin in the garden of Eden: that man shall not live by bread alone but by every word from God.

> But he answered and said, "It is written, 'Man shall not live by bread alone, but by every word that proceedeth out of the mouth of God.'"
>
> Matthew 4:4 (KJV)

I believe this should have been Adam and Eve's response to the serpent when he told them to eat of the forbidden fruits. Here in this scriptural reference, it is suggesting that mankind should not live by food only. There are two things that are required for mankind to live: bread, meaning food, and the Word of God, meaning the Bible. Food is for the physical nourishment and growth of the body. Anyone who does not want to eat food for the proper development of their body will become deformed and will eventually die of starvation. Likewise, the Word of God is spiritual nourishment for the spirit and soul. Failure to feed the spiritual man will cause a deformity of the spirit and soul and its eventual death. Anyone who does not feed on the Word of God by reading the Bible, praying, and worshiping God will become spiritually deformed and will die spiritually by being separated or alienated from God (spiritual death).

WHAT IS THE FORBIDDEN FRUIT?

So, what really happened in the garden? Did not God say that everything he created was good and that he was pleased with his creation?

> And God saw everything that he had made, and, behold, it was very good. And the evening and the morning were the sixth day.
>
> Genesis 1:31 (KJV)

So why did God tell Adam and Eve "...of every tree you may freely eat, but the tree of knowledge of good and evil, you shall not eat of it, for the day that you eat of it you will surely die" (Genesis 2:17, KJV). Why? Was the tree spoiled, poisonous, or bad for them to eat? No, because Genesis 1:31 states that everything God created was very good. So why? Was there anything mystical about this particular tree that God singled out from all his creation? I believe there was nothing mystical about this particular tree. I believe this is where God made three things known to man: First, he made known to man their free will; this is where God first gave mankind their choice, the ability to choose him (life) or death (sin). Second, this is where God tested man's obedience or faithfulness to him. And last, this is where God declared His sovereignty over mankind and over all of creation, which he had made. If the tree of good and evil was spoiled or poisonous or bad for them, what was it doing in the beautiful garden? The sin of mankind or the rebellion of mankind was more than just eating of the tree of knowledge or the forbidden fruit. In order to see this revelation, we have to understand what Scripture teaches about fruits. Therefore, let us list some scriptural references about fruits:

> Beware of false prophets, which come to you in sheep's clothing, but inwardly they are ravening wolves. Ye shall know them by their fruits. Do men gather grapes of thorns, or figs of thistles? Even so every good tree bringeth forth good fruit; but a corrupt tree bringeth forth evil fruit. A good tree cannot bring forth evil fruit, neither can a corrupt tree bring forth good fruit. Every tree that bringeth not forth good fruit is hewn down, and cast into the fire. Wherefore by their fruits ye shall know them.
>
> Matthew 7:15-20 (KJV)

In this reference, we see false prophets disguising themselves in sheep's clothing, but in their hearts, they are wolves. The Bible states you shall know them by their doings (fruits). Thus, fruits (characters) are the result of our behavior based on the knowledge we have. Thus, we do the things we do because of the knowledge we have. Humans are governed by knowledge (intelligence); animals are governed by instinct.

> Blessed is the man that walketh not in the counsel of the ungodly, nor standeth in the way of sinners, nor sitteth in the seat of the scornful. But his delight is in the law of the Lord; and in his law doth he meditate day and night. And he shall be like a tree planted by the rivers of water, that

bringeth forth his fruit in his season; his leaf also shall not wither; and whatsoever he doeth shall prosper.

Psalm 1:1-3 (KJV)

In this scriptural reference, we see that a man who mediates on God's laws day and night will be like trees planted by the rivers of water that bring forth fruits (good character) in his season and will prosper in everything that he does.

> Great in counsel, and mighty in work: for thine eyes are open upon all the ways of the sons of men: to give everyone according to his ways, and according to the fruit (character/action) of his doings...
>
> Jeremiah 32:19 (KJV)

> Death and life are in the power of the tongue: and they that love it shall eat the fruit thereof.
>
> Proverbs 18:21 (KJV)

> Say ye to the righteous, that it shall be well with him: for they shall eat the fruit of their doings.
>
> Isaiah 3:10 (KJV)

> Hear, O earth: behold, I will bring evil upon this people, even the fruit of their thoughts, because they have not hearkened unto my words, nor to my law, but rejected it.
>
> Jeremiah 6:19 (KJV)

> I the Lord search the heart, I try the reins, even to give every man according to his ways, and according to the fruit of his doings.
>
> Jeremiah 17:10 (KJV)

> Bring forth therefore fruits worthy of repentance, and begin not to say within yourselves, We have Abraham to our father: for I say unto you, That God is able of these stones to raise up children unto Abraham.
>
> Luke 3:8 (KJV)

In this scriptural reference, we see John the Baptist telling the religious leaders to bring fruit (behavior /action) that is worthy of God's forgiveness. It is not good to say and not do. Our behavior or actions can lead us to hell, the eternal fire, says the next reference:

> And now also the axe is laid unto the root of the trees: every tree therefore which bringeth not forth good fruit is hewn down, and cast into the fire.
>
> Luke 3:9 (KJV)

Hence this revelation: if the tree of knowledge of good and evil or the forbidden fruit was not also metaphorical, according to this scripture, this tree should have been cut down and thrown into the fire.

> Every branch in me that beareth not fruit he taketh away: and every branch that beareth fruit, he purgeth it, that it may bring forth more fruit.
>
> John 15:2 (KJV)

> Abide in me, and I in you. As the branch cannot bear fruit of itself, except it abide in the vine; no more can ye, except ye abide in me. I am the vine, ye are the branches: He that abideth in me, and I in him, the same bringeth forth much fruit: for without me ye can do nothing.
>
> John 15:4-5 (KJV)

In this scriptural reference, we see that without Jesus Christ, we cannot bear good fruits. He is the tree, and we are the branches, and since we are in him, we are able to bring forth good fruit, but without him, we cannot do anything.

> Herein is my Father glorified, that ye bear much fruit; so shall ye be my disciples.
>
> John 15:8 (KJV)

In this scriptural reference, we see that the Father is glorified through us producing good fruits. Our behavior or deeds (fruit) will determine whether we are Jesus Christ's disciples.

So we see through these scriptural references that a fruit, throughout Scripture, is an act, deed, knowledge and behavior of the individual. Thus, the principle is that human beings govern themselves based on or according to the knowledge (fruits) he or she has. We do the things we do based on the knowledge we have. If people believed that they could fly, they would go on the roof of a building and dare try. Since they know they cannot fly, they govern themselves accordingly, based on the knowledge they have. A person that knows they cannot swim will not dare jump into a sixteen-foot pool because they know they could drown. They govern themselves according to their knowledge or what they know. In the book of Hosea, it states that people perished because of lack of knowledge.

> My people are destroyed for lack of knowledge: because thou hast rejected knowledge, I will also reject thee, that thou shalt be no priest to me: seeing thou hast forgotten the law of thy God, I will also forget thy children.
>
> Hosea 4:6 (KJV)

You see, the reason why God's children die is because they don't have proper knowledge of God. Why? Because the god of this world has blinded them with darkness so they will not see the light of God which is the truth, knowledge that frees and liberates us from death and, most importantly, frees us from the grip of the enemy. Knowledge of God liberates us; any other knowledge apart from God is sin and it breeds or brings death. For example, knowledge of Satan keeps us in darkness, captivity, or bondage and separates us from the knowledge of God. So, people are dying because they don't have or know the Word of God; the truth which sets us free or that brings or breeds life. Therefore, forbidden fruit is forbidden knowledge or knowledge that is forbidden which is knowledge of Satan or satanic activities such as witchcraft, sorcery, voodoo, black magic, etc. On that note, let me give you the spiritual meaning behind what happened in the garden. The tree of knowledge of good and evil was a symbol of Satan, for he was created good but did not remain good by a willful choice he made. The tree of life is a symbol of Jesus Christ, for he is the life giver and knowledge of him will yield eternal life. Adam and Eve disobedience to God cause them to sin.

However, when it said they took of the forbidden fruit and ate, it was metaphorically stating that Adam and Eve accepted Satan's knowledge and disregarded the knowledge God gave them previously about not eating from the tree of knowledge of good and evil. Now hint this revelation it was simply suggesting that they stood under the counsel of Satan and embraced the knowledge (fruit) that Satan had to offer by partaking of the fruit which was forbidden. Satan imparted knowledge in them and when they embraced that knowledge, it brought about death (separation). Therefore, it was the knowledge (fruit) Adam and Eve gained that brought about death. Because this knowledge, the knowledge of Satan, altered their behavior, affected their spiritual ability to communicate with God and their spiritual eyes were closed; they became fearful. Why fearful? Because when they accepted Satan's knowledge, it stripped them of their confidence in God. They could no longer see God and his protective angels; they could only hear God. They became spiritually blinded, no longer had the capacity or ability to walk and live in the spiritual realm; they became carnal, self-seeking or selfishness. By accepting Satan's knowledge over God, they embraced the spirit of fear, weakness, hate, and unstableness of mind, as opposed to what God said he did not give us:

> For God hath not given us the spirit of fear; but of power, and of love, and of a sound mind.
>
> 2 Timothy 1:7 (KJV)

Did not Adam say he was fearful because he was naked (Genesis 3:10, KJV)? They were defeated and tormented, and their physical eyes were opened; as a result, they began to govern themselves according to what they saw (sight) as opposed to walking and living by faith; the scriptures are clear concerning this principle:

> For we walk by faith, not by sight...
>
> 2 Corinthians 5:7 (KJV)

Adam and Eve accepting Satan's knowledge altered the harmonious balance of man by causing the order of man to be changed. This rotated the order of man from spirit, soul and body (flesh) to body (flesh), soul, and spirit; the body (flesh) became the dominant part of our being. This is one of the reasons that Jesus Christ came, to give us back our life by putting into order or to reverse this order back to spirit, soul, and body.

God was right and Satan was wrong because Adam and Eve did die that very day. Satan lied to them and said they would not surely die. Here is scriptural proof that Adam and Eve died that day. Scripture teaches that one day to God is a thousand years and a thousand years to God is as one day. Because Adam lived till he was 930 years old and did not live past a thousand years, he did not even live a day. So according to God, they died that very day.

> But, beloved, be not ignorant of this one thing, that one day is with the Lord as a thousand years, and a thousand years as one day.
>
> 2 Peter 3:8 (KJV)

Remember that we see many references of what fruit is in the spiritual realm.

I stumbled upon this revelation based on a doubt I had, which might be the same doubt some of you might have had or still have. I used to constantly say to myself after reading the book of Genesis, *How can the whole of creation die because of just eating a fruit?* This doubt led me to study the scriptures intensively, regarding what they teach about a fruit. I highlighted this revelation in my first book, *His Name Is Not God*. It was their disobedience of rejecting God knowledge and their acceptance of Satan knowledge that brought death into the human world.

Satan successfully obtained or stole Adam's crown. It did not cost him anything; in fact, it gained him a kingdom. Satan was after Adam, not Eve; he used Eve to get to Adam because the crown or dominion was given to Adam. I have come to see that this type of deception is one of Satan's most powerful schemes; when he uses women to get to the men. This why some of the greatest men of God have fallen at the hands of Satan because he is able to influence the women into indirectly bringing down their husband or any powerful men of God. We see this master deception throughout the scriptures, like Adam and Eve, Samson and Delilah, King David and Bathsheba, etc. Remember the story of Job, how the scriptures say that Job was perfect and upright, a man that feared God and hated evil. Remember the very thing that Satan said Job would do if God stopped blessing him and stopped protecting him—that he would curse God to the face and die. God gave Satan the permission to take everything Job had to see if Job would curse God. Immediately, we see, Satan went to work, destroying all Job had; he killed his children, killed all his livestock, his servants, and destroyed his farm. Everything that Job had, Satan took away, except for his wife; he did not touch his wife. This was his master plan, to preserve the one that was closest to him in hopes of influencing her to do his bidding against Job. Finally, we witness that Job's wife told Job to curse God and die, the very bet Satan had with God. Job still maintaining his integrity, he would not lift his voice to curse God but would rather curse the day he was born. The wife told Job to curse God and die, and Job told her she was a foolish woman to even think that (Job 2:1-10, KJV). Job's wife did not have integrity and one can safely assume that she was only with Job for his wealth and riches. She would be what one could classify as a gold digger. She was Satan's pawn to try and destroy Job just like how Satan used Eve to get to Adam. This is why I believe Scripture cautions the husbands to dwell with our wives according to knowledge and wash them with the Word of God. We, as husbands must be able to come against the influence of the enemy upon our wives' lives, being mindful of the seeds or the negative thoughts that the enemy is planting in their heads against us, prohibiting the men of God walking in his calling. Good thing Job did not give in to Satan's pawn because he could have lost his salvation. Job is my hero; he is a good example of how to trust God no matter what.

Satan's influence caused Adam and Eve to eat the forbidden fruits; his corrupt actions was an act of defilement against God. It sent a clear statement to God of his intension to steal, kill, and destroy all that he has here on earth, since he can't get to God in heaven. Satan's plan is to destroy all those who possess the image of God, or act like God, producing good fruits (character). I can imagine Satan standing on earth and looking up toward heaven, where he fell from his two fists beating his chest along with his angels in rejoicing over their victory over Adam and Eve (mankind) by indirectly causing them to join their rebellion against God. And with this victory, he set course to make this earth their kingdom.

This temporary victory over Adam and Eve strengthened his pride. I can now imagine him saying, "He sent a boy to do a man's job, giving the boy dominion over us; yeah, that's why I tricked them and took their dominion away from them. Now they will have to serve and worship me." Father God, looking down from heaven, saw what happened and was not surprised because he knew what was going to happen. He had already made provision for mankind to deliver them from the grip of Satan and his demons. So God came down in the cool of the day and confronted and sentenced each one of them. Satan was sentenced to be bruised to the head which is a symbol of death. Eve's sentence was pain during child birth and Adam was sentenced to hard labor. He punished each one according to his righteous judgments. God sent man and his wife out of Eden, out of his presence, to earth, where they were created. God felt divorced, alienated from earth, as the only representative he had on earth to carry out his will was now captive unknowingly. As judge of the earth and all things in heaven and earth, he punishes, condemns, all those who do not do his will.

> Daniel answered and said, blessed be the name of God for ever and ever: for wisdom and might are his: And he changeth the times and the seasons: he removeth kings, and setteth up kings: he giveth wisdom unto the wise, and knowledge to them that know understanding: He revealeth the deep and secret things: he knoweth what is in the darkness, and the light dwelleth with him. I thank thee, and praise thee, O thou God of my fathers, who hast given me wisdom and might, and hast made known unto me now what we desired of thee: for thou hast now made known unto us the king's matter.
>
> Daniel 2:20-23 (KJV)

So, when God evicted or expelled man and his wife out to the garden of Eden, guess who was waiting for them at the exit of Eden, welcoming them to their new home—Satan and all his fallen angels. This was really the time Adam and Eve were truly lonely because they were now in this vast wilderness in comparison to the garden of Eden. I know they regretted their choice and would give anything just to have fellowship with God again; this realization could only come to those who have tasted and seen how good God is. I know they missed their relationship with God, their Father, friend, mentor, guidance, comforter, confidant, etc. Satan became the new prince of earth or the god of this world.

Now that Satan had managed to usurp Adam's dominion, his plan is to establish his kingdom here on earth where he can be exalted as god by implementing a world government that would allow mankind to directly or indirectly accept him as king or god over the kingdom of man. Thus, through the process of time, a democratic system was born. This new government was going to incorporate all other earthly government, uniting of all world leaders and their governments in hopes of establishing a new world order, one world government that would be influence by Satan and his demons. This new world order is the system of one world government (the beast), one world religion (the false prophets) and one world monetary system (economic and financial resources). This is one of the reasons why there is a great spread of democracy throughout the world. Those world leaders or governments that do not change or convert to this democratic regime will be deposed and overthrown and another leader will be put in their place that will abide by the democratic system of governments; slowly and shortly, the whole world will be under a democratic system. Along with democratizing the world, there is also a false sense of conversion of religion. One of the rules of war is that whoever wins will set up their god over the captives or the land or country that has been invaded or deposed. All this conflict within our world today, particularly the conflict between the West and the East will only result in one victor and whoever the victor is will establish their god that will rule the whole world as the god who brought them victory.

Once this is accomplished, the next task or agenda is to get rid of all Christians, those who are called by God's name, those who stand for Jesus Christ or preach in his name. Yes, what I am saying is there is going to be a great persecution of Christians throughout the whole world. This great persecution is the implementation or the institution of the mark of the beast, where he will cause great, small, free, bonded, etc. to receive the mark of the beast.

> And he causeth all, both small and great, rich and poor, free and bond, to receive a mark in their right hand, or in their foreheads: And that no man might buy or sell, save he that had the mark, or the name of the beast, or the number of his name.
> Here is wisdom. Let him that hath understanding count the number of the beast: for it isthe number of a man; and his number is Six hundred threescore and six
>
> Revelation 13:16-18 (KJV)

Satan does not want any light in his kingdom because he is the prince of darkness. Therefore, he does not want Christians (Christ-like), who are the light of the world, in his kingdom. Therefore, there will be a great deception going on.

> For there shall arise false Christ's, and false prophets, and shall show great signs and wonders; insomuch that, if it were possible, they shall deceive the very elect.
>
> Matthew 24:24 (KJV)

Jesus Christ said a bad tree cannot bear a good fruit and neither can a good tree bear a bad fruits. What I am saying is that you cannot put a wicked person in power and expect them to produce good fruits or a good kingdom. Only a righteous king can produce a good kingdom by promoting righteousness, good conduct, peace, prosperity, fruitfulness, etc. In fact, when the wicked are in authority, they kill and destroy the kingdom. They lack vision and therefore abuse the power given to them; as a result, the citizens or the people suffer or will be destroyed. They will impose unlawful burdens on the people and haul all excess for themselves and their loyal servants, leaving the citizen depraved, poor, and destitute. There is always a great outcry when the wicked advance in power.

CHRISTIAN NATION
WHAT CONSTITUTES A CHRISTIAN NATION?

Just because you call yourself a Christian does not necessarily mean you are a Christian. Just because you carry your Bible under your arm everywhere you go does not mean you read it. A Christian is one who not only reads the Bible but believes it and lives by it. This principle also applies to any states, countries, nations, or kingdoms that profess to be a Christian nation. You could profess with your mouth all you want and rant about being a Christian nation or a Christian county, but if you fail to live up the standards of the Bible, it is all lip service, and the truth is not in you or in your country or nation. In fact, scriptures call such behavior hypocrisy:

> He answered and said unto them, "Well hath Esaias prophesied of you hypocrites, as it is written, This people honoureth me with their lips, but their heart is far from me. Howbeit in vain do they worship me, teaching for doctrines the commandments of men?"
>
> Mark 7:6-7 (KJV)

It does not matter whether a country or nation has written documents in their constitution or laws that express, quote, or reference God; if they fail to let God govern it, it is only a forged document; a letter that kills. It does not matter whether that they have Bibles within their courts systems that they use to administer oaths; if the judges or the law makers themselves does not read the Bible, how can they know what is written in it to determine a fair and rightful judgment or what kind of judgment one should be judged by? How can they rightly judge you if they themselves do not keep the rules and regulations stated in the Bible? If one does not have fear or reverence for the Bible, why make the Bible the standard by which one takes oaths? Atheists will certainly not have a problem swearing on the Bible because they don't believe in the Bible or God. Because they don't read it and they have no fear for God. Therefore, their testimony are often false when they swear in court on the bible, so as a result we have a system that is broken and have put innocence people in jail and some they have executed through capital punishment. This is a deception influence by Satan the so called the god of this world upon the forefathers who broke away from their previous government to establish a state separated from any religious affiliation. Why am I constantly mentioning the Bible? Why the Bible? Because the codification of a Christian or a Christian nation is predicated on the ability to be governed by the Bible, by reasons of believing it is divine in origination and inspired by God, for correction, reproof, and instruction in righteousness.

> All scripture is given by inspiration of God, and is profitable for doctrine, for reproof, for correction, for instruction in righteousness: That the man of God may be perfect, thoroughly furnished unto all good works.
>
> 2 Timothy 3:16-17 (KJV)

What then constitutes a Christian nation? A Christian nation is a nation or kingdom whose people and government have made Jesus Christ, their Lord and Savior, the divine entity that governs its people and government. Therefore, they bear his name, Christian nation or Christlike nation. A Christlike nation or Christian nation is a nation that believes in one God (monotheism). That means they do not tolerate or condone or compromise any other religion or any worship to any other god that does not bring glory and honor to the true God, Jesus Christ. That means no other religion is practiced within that nation or kingdom because it breeds idolatry and will violate God's commandments. We see a numereous references in the old testament to nations or kingdoms that were monotheistic was strict about who and what they worship. The consequence of anyone within the nation or kingdom worshiping or paying tributes to other gods was death by stoning.

> Now Samuel was dead, and all Israel had lamented him, and buried him in Ramah, even in his own city. And Saul had put away those that had familiar spirits, and the wizards, out of the land.
>
> 1 Samuel 28:3 (KJV)

A Christlike nation is a theocratic nation whose deity is the Lord Jesus Christ, meaning he is the spiritual entity that influences that kingdom or government. Christian nations are disciples or followers of Jesus Christ who seek to advance God's kingdom by going throughout the world preaching and teaching the gospel (good news) in love, not in war. Christian nations abide by the strict teachings of Jesus Christ by loving one's enemy, doing good to those who despitefully use them, praying for their enemy, turning the other cheek, and simply by winning people to Jesus Christ to become their Lord and Savior through love, the greatest gift of all. You cannot have a democracy and then call your country a Christian nation, because democracy is governed according to the will of the people as opposed to the kingdom of God/Christ, which is the will of the king that prevails. In a Christ like nation, the Ten Commandments are honored, it is the rule of law that governs the entire nation. In democratic systems, the Ten Commandments are split between two parties, the Democrats and the Republicans. Each party takes one or half of the commandments and makes it their code of honor or moral conviction by which they judge and condemn all things, negating or ignoring the rest of the commandments. These two parties are responsible for making sure all the citizens of their nation fall under at least one party. Whatever party the citizen strongly identifies with in respect to their moral convictions will be the party they will join or generally vote for. These parties remind me of the Pharisees and the Sadducees, two primary groups in Jesus's time who kept on challenging Jesus and were constantly being put to shame by Jesus Christ. For instance, one party will heavily push their prolife agenda while at the same time voting for war or condoning capital punishment. The other party will present its convictions on more government control for business accountability and less privacy for the citizens which slowly strips away our freedom. They split and divide the people into two groups and bombard them with their half commandments, because they know that society is commandment driven, that no one in their right mind would argue against killing, abortion, stealing, murder, etc. Therefore, one can safely say that democracy violates and offends all that is God, especially the Ten Commandments because scriptures teaches if you guilty of one of the laws of you are guilty of all of them. In a democratic system, the citizens or people are free to worship and practice whatever religion or gods they choose which they call freedom of religion. The price of this freedom that democracy gives is at the expense of one's soul because you are free worship Satan, practice witchcraft, voodoo, etc, which is all forbidden by God. Any Christ-like nation or Christian nation will not tolerate this concept or ideology. How can one's country or nation consider itself as a Christian nation when they steal people (slavery) and kill innocence people (Indians) in the name of their god, a false god they think is God? You might ask yourself, *How did my country or my nation steal and kill innocent people?* By stealing and ripping innocent people from their families and forcing them into free labor through the importation of slavery and by stealing the land from the native people (Indians) and practically bringing the native people to the brink of extinction. The country or nation that call themselves a Christian nation credits their god; the god of democracy, for the victories over the lives of those they conquered and enslaved. The god of democracy goes around deceiving and blaspheming the noble name of God, portraying itself to the world as a Christian nation or a Christlike nation, tainting the image and name of God through identity theft, creating havoc throughout the world in the name of Christianity, the second greatest deception known to mankind. This is why Satan himself is said to transform into an angel of light.

> And no marvel; for Satan himself is transformed into an angel of light. Therefore, it is no great thing if his ministers also be transformed as the ministers of righteousness; whose end shall be according to their works.
>
> 2 Corinthians 11:14-15 (KJV)

SHOULD CHRISTIANS GO TO WAR?

Should Christians go to war? This is a question I often ask Christians and especially pastors. The answer varies from pastor to pastor but never on what the scriptures teaches about war. I believe comprehension of this biblical truth will lead us to rightly interpret the scriptures. In order for us to understand the nature of this question, we must seek to understand the totality of Scripture; in that way, our interpretation and conclusion is biblically based. Let us first define *Christian. A Christian is one who is a follower or a disciple of Jesus Christ. The follower is seeking to be like Christ, or Christlike.* What is *war? "A war is armed conflict between states or nations (international war) or between factions within a state (civil war), prosecuted by force and having the purpose of compelling the defeated side to do the will of the victor"* (http:// en.wikipedia.org/wiki/War). A good biblical example of the defeated doing the will of the victor in the time of war would be

> In the third year of the reign of Jehoiakim king of Judah came Nebuchadnezzar king of Babylon unto Jerusalem, and besieged it. And the Lord gave Jehoiakim king of Judah into his hand, with part of the vessels of the house of God: which he carried into the land of Shinar to the house of his god; and he brought the vessels into the treasure house of his god.
>
> Daniel 1:1-5 (KJV)

Now that we know the nature of what war is, let examine the scriptures to find out where wars come from.

> ...from whence come wars and fighting among you? come they not hence, even of your lusts that war in your members?
>
> James 4:1 (KJV)

> For from within, out of the heart of men, proceed evil thoughts, adulteries, fornications, murders, Thefts, covetousness, wickedness, deceit, lasciviousness, an evil eye, blasphemy, pride, foolishness: All these evil things come from within, and defile the man.
>
> Mark 7:21-23 (KJV)

In this portion of Scripture, Jesus explains the difference between food eaten with unwashed hands and the words we speak; he concludes that the words we speak are what defile, hinder, discourage, assassinate, etc. a man. He stated that eating with unwashed hands does not defile a man, but the words that come out of the mouth do. Why? Because mankind in general is held accountable by two things: words and actions.

Our words will determine our actions; our actions are a result of our words which are part of the decision-making process or the choices we make. Our thoughts (words) formulate our beliefs; it is from our beliefs that we make choices or decisions, our choices lead to our actions or behavior and our behavior will determine our fate or destiny. Therefore, the choices of our words will determine our actions and our actions are a result of our words. For example, a person who has a good reputation of keeping his word is held accountable or judged by his word or actions. Someone who is inconsistent in his words or actions is also judged by his words or action; therefore, one can conclude that he or she is not a man or woman of their word. People in general would have a hard time trusting or believing in him or her. So, based on these assumptions, they are characterized by their words or actions. If the president of the United States addressed the nation and stated, "We are declaring war with a specific nation or country," the United States Army, Navy, Marines, Air force, etc., would have to immediately act on his words because the words we speak force us to take action. As another example, consider an average person that threatens to kill or assassinate another. Law enforcement would undoubtedly question him or her to determine his or her motives. Words have creative power; it's through words that nations, states, and countries declare war against one another and their subsequent actions validate their words. Most wars are caused by ideology, politics, racism, and economic and religious conflicts (http://en.wikipedia.org/wiki/War).

TESTAMENT

In attempting to understand the totality of the Bible in regard to war, we must consider understanding the Old and the New Testaments. The two simpler ways to understand the Old and New Testaments are to understand the dispensation of the Law and the dispensation of grace. But before I explain what dispensation is, let me explain what a testament is. A testament is often used in biblical interpretation as a covenant between God and men. So, in essence, the Old

Testament is a covenant between God and the children of Israel to keep his laws that he gave to Moses. The New Testament is God fulfilling his promises of the old covenants by putting his laws into the heart and mind of his people (The Children of Israel). The Old Testament is a covenant by which God redeems the children of Israel for himself, out of all other people or nations. The New Testament is a covenant where God saves his people, children of Israel. However, the dictionary defines *testament* as *an act by which a person determines the disposition (transferable) of his or her property after death*. In further understanding the two covenants, I will dare say that Psalm 24:1-2 (KJV) is the testament or will by which God intends to give earth to his elect chosen people (mankind).

> The earth is the Lord and the fullness thereof; the world and they that dwell therein, for He had founded it upon the sea, and established it upon the floods.
>
> Psalm 24:1-2 (KJV)

The essences of these covenants or testaments is to one day give mankind all of earth through the shed blood of Jesus Christ who created all things in heaven and on earth. But only to those who are worthy of him, his choice people, or chosen people, shall inherit the earth, which are the saved, or the meek.

> Blessed are the meek: for they shall inherit the earth.
>
> Matthew 5:5 (KJV)

How are they going to inherit the earth? This is why we see that the death of our Lord and Savior Jesus Christ was so crucial in terms of 1) restoring mankind back to eternal life, 2) restoring earth back to its original purpose, for we know that Satan had made earth into a wilderness, and 3) to restore earth back to mankind who lost it through the deception of the enemy. So Jesus Christ's death was not only for the restoration of mankind but also for the restoration of earth and its return back to mankind dominion. How else is mankind going to inherit earth if Jesus Christ had not died for them to inherit it? By Jesus Christ's death, we are redeemed from the curse of the Law and are given eternal life. By Jesus Christ's death, earth will one day be restored back to its original purpose.

> And for this cause he is the mediator of the new testament, that by means of death, for the redemption of the transgressions that were under the first testament, they which are called might receive the promise of eternal inheritance. For where a testament is, there must also of necessity be the death of the testator.
>
> Hebrew 9:15-22 (KJV)

A *testator* is defined as "*a person who has written and executed a last will and testament that is in effect at the time of his or her death; it is any "person" who makes a will*". http://en.wikipedia.org/wiki/ Testator Therefore, if it is God's intention to give all of earth to mankind, it now makes sense as to why he had to die—so that we can inherit earth.

"In certain religions, a dispensation is a distinctive arrangement or period in history that forms the framework through which God relates to mankind". (http://en.wikipedia.org/wiki/ Dispensation_(period) There are two dispensations that pertain to the covenants or testaments: the dispensation of the Law and the dispensation of grace; these two testaments constitute the whole Bible. There are numerous scriptures that help explain or clarify these testaments or covenants.

> For the law was given by Moses, but grace and truth came by Jesus Christ.
>
> John 1:17 (KJV)

> "Behold, the days come," saith the Lord, "that I will make a new covenant with the house of Israel, and with the house of Judah: Not according to the covenant that I made with their fathers in the day that I took them by the hand to bring them out of the land of Egypt; which my covenant they brake, although I was an husband unto them," saith the Lord:
>
> Jeremiah 31:31-33 (KJV)

Therefore, under the dispensation of the Law, God dealt with a particular group of people called the children of Israel.

Under the dispensation of the Law:
- It was an eye for an eye, a tooth for a tooth
- the Law condemned you

Under the dispensation of Grace:
- It's no longer an eye for eye or a tooth for a tooth
- The Law no longer condemns you
- Grace forgives you

We get a glimpse of this biblical truth of how grace overshadows or overpowers the Law because the Law wanted to condemn the woman who was caught in adultery but grace wanted to forgive her; grace convicts, not condemns.

> And the scribes and Pharisees brought unto him a woman taken in adultery; and when they had set her in the midst, they say unto him, "Master, this woman was taken in adultery, in the very act. Now Moses in the Law commanded us that such should be stoned: but what sayest thou?" This they said, tempting him, that they might have to accuse him. But Jesus stooped down, and with his finger wrote on the ground, as though he heard them not.
>
> John 8:3-11 (KJV)

As we examine this portion of Scripture, we see that one main reason the woman was not condemned by the Law was because grace was merciful; even though she deserved to be stoned to death, grace would not allow her to be condemned. In examining the text, we notice that she was improperly accused, even though she was caught red-handed committing adultery. To understand this truth, we must try to understand what Jesus Christ wrote on the ground. What did he write? I believe he wrote on the ground the answer to their question, which they kept asking him, saying, "Moses said if anyone is caught in adultery they out to be stoned, but what do you say?" (John 8:1-11, KJV) So Jesus stooped to the ground and wrote, "So where is the man? You brought the woman; what happened to the man?"

Even though Scripture does not reveal what he wrote on the ground, through understanding the totality of the Bible, one can safely assume that he wrote this on the ground: "Where is the man?" I believe this is what he wrote on the ground, because based on:

> And the man that committeth adultery with another man's wife, even he that committeth adultery with his neighbour's wife, the adulterer and the adulteress shall surely be put to death.
>
> Leviticus 20:10 (KJV)

You cannot condemn the woman without also condemning the man. Why? Because it takes two to commit adultery; the woman did not commit adultery by herself, so why did they only bring the woman and not the man? After all the accusers left, Jesus stood up and said, "Hath no man condemned you?" And she said, "No man, Lord." Jesus replied and said, "Neither do I condemn you; go and sin no more." Even though Jesus had every right to condemn her because she directly sinned against him; he gave her grace, which is God's unmeritible favor. When King David was convicted of adultery, his prayer of forgiveness was this:

> Against thee, thee only, have I sinned, and done this evil in thy sight: that thou mightest be justified when thou speakest, and be clear when thou judgest.
>
> Psalm 51:4 (KJV)

Now what does all of this have to do with Christians going to war? It is important that we understand what dispensation we are in; in that way, we can determine God's will for us. Under the dispensation of grace, we are no longer under the Law, an eye for eye and a tooth for tooth and no longer are God's chosen people only the Jews but are all those who have accepted Jesus Christ as Lord and Savior. We no longer call for war but for peace; we are no longer called to hate our enemies but to love our enemies, to do good to them that hate us, to bless those who curse us and to pray for those who spitefully used us (Luke 6:27-32, 35,36, KJV).

And the only thing that our Lord Jesus Christ asks of us under the dispensation of grace is to go into the entire world and teach and baptize them in the name of the Father, the Son, and the Holy Ghost (Matthew 28:18-20, KJV).

This is what our Lord and Savior is asking of us, not to war against one another. In fact, the only warfare he calls us to is spiritual warfare where we put on the whole armor of God so that we can stand against the wiles of the devil. For we fight not against flesh and blood but against principalities, against powers, against rulers of darkness in this world and against spiritual wickedness in high places.

> Finally, my brethren, be strong in the Lord, and in the power of his might. Put on the whole armour of God, that ye may be able to stand against the wiles of the devil. For we wrestle not against flesh and blood, but against

> principalities, against powers, against the rulers of the darkness of this world, against spiritual wickedness in high places.
>
> Ephesians 6:10-18 (KJV)

CHRISTIANS KILLING CHRISTIANS

In fact, Jesus himself said if his kingdom was of this world, his servant would have fought for him so that he would not have been delivered to them.

> Jesus answered, "My kingdom is not of this world: if my kingdom were of this world, then would my servants fight, that I should not be delivered to the Jews: but now is my kingdom not from hence."
>
> John 18:36 (KJV)

This is to show that whatever kingdom you are more loyal to, you will fight to defend. Imagine me, a Christian expressing more loyalty to my country than to my God and I heeded the call to war against another country. And, let's say, the country we are going to war with also has Christians within their nation and they are also more loyal to their country than to God and heeded the call to go war against my country. The result is you will have Christians killing Christians on the battlefield. This is a great deception; the enemy has managed to deceive Christians that this is a Christian nation, so we must fight for God. Yes, the Bible says obey the law of the land but not if the law of the land violates or hinders our walk or relationship with God. We should not honor that request. Two examples illustrate this reasoning. First, Shadrack, Meshach, and Abednego failed to obey the law of the land by not bowing down to the statue King Nebuchadnezzar erected because it violated God's commandments.

> Shadrach, Meshach, and Abednego, answered and said to the king, "O Nebuchadnezzar, we are not careful to answer thee in this matter. If it be so, our God whom we serve is able to deliver us from the burning fiery furnace, and he will deliver us out of thine hand, O king. But if not, be it known unto thee, O king, that we will not serve thy gods, nor worship the golden image which thou hast set up."
>
> Daniel 3:16-23 (KJV)

Second, Daniel, who refused to obey the law of the land by not praying to his God for at least thirty days because it would hinder his relationship with God, was thrown in the lion's den (Daniel 6:6-22, KJV).

We as Christians must obey the law of the land as long as it does not violate or hinder our relationship with God or interfere with God's laws. We are supposed to be only loyal to the kingdom of God; it is the kingdom of God that governs us Christians and not the kingdom of this world. Even though Satan is the god of this world, he does not control or govern God's children or sons. It was Jesus Christ that died for you and me so that we could be free from the rudiments of this world and from the wickedness of this world. If Jesus Christ's disciples or followers did not fight for Jesus Christ, why should I or we as Christians, fight for Caesar and his government or any other government to establish their anti-kingdom? Jesus Christ prays that we stay true to his Word so that we will not become part of this world because we are not of this world, and because we are not of this world, the world hates us.

> I have given them thy word; and the world hath hated them, because they are not of the world, even as I am not of the world. I pray not that thou shouldest take them out of the world, but that thou shouldest keep them from the evil. They are not of the world, even as I am not of the world.
>
> John 17:14-19 (KJV)

If this is true, that the world will hate us because we are Christians or of Christ or not of this world, does it make sense to fight for it? These thoughts and concepts remind me of the slavery of the African people in America; how they went to war and fought to help liberate their oppressor, thinking that they were also fighting for their independence yet they were still hated by their oppressor, and their oppressor continued to enslave them. The law of the land not only violated African American slaves in America, it also violated God's laws. Whose war did they fight? Who was really their enemy, the people they fought against or the people who continuously oppressed them and refused to let them exercise their rights as a human being? In fact, I will go as far as to say that when we are more loyal to our earthly king than to our heavenly King, we diminish and indirectly reject Jesus Christ, our true King, the King of kings. The children of Israel fell into this category when they indirectly rejected God as their king and requested for an earthly king to rule them. This request not only displeased Samuel but was heartbreaking for God; nevertheless, God came and told Samuel to give those stubborn people bent on following false gods what they want, for they have not rejected Samuel but have rejected Him as being king over them.

> And it came to pass, when Samuel was old, that he made his sons judges over Israel. Now the name of his firstborn was Joel; and the name of his second, Abiah: they were judges in Beersheba. And his sons walked not in his ways, but turned aside after lucre, and took bribes, and perverted judgment.
>
> 1 Samuel 8:1-7 (KJV)

They rejected God as the spiritual king that should rule and govern them. It was for this reason that God appeared in human form as Jesus Christ, they again rejected him openly and told him to his face that they only had one king, and that was Caesar.

> And it was the preparation of the passover, and about the sixth hour: and he saith unto the Jews, "Behold your King!" But they cried out, "Away with him, away with him, crucify him." Pilate saith unto them, "Shall I crucify your King?" The chief priests answered, "We have no king but Caesar."
>
> John 19:14-15 (KJV)

Why is not being part of the world so important to Jesus Christ? Because the world is under condemnation and judgment by God. The world is a type of Egypt that puts people in bondage, captivity, or slavery and Jesus Christ came as a deliverer to deliver us from Satan who is a modernday pharaoh, the king of a worldly slavery system. This is the same scenario as when God, through the burning bush, bid Moses to go tell the pharaoh to let his people go so that they could worship him in the wilderness. So when the fullness of time came, God sent forth his only begotten Son to come and deliver his people from this worldly slavery system so that we could worship Him through Jesus Christ. The world, as we know, hates Jesus Christ, so they will also hate those who follower him. So why should I fight to defend a kingdom that hates my God, the Father and Creator of heaven and earth who came to free me so I won't have to fight or study war anymore? This is why the world hates us Christians, because we are followers of Jesus Christ; in fact, Jesus warned us and said that the world would hates us because we love him. Satan is seeking to establish his anti-kingdoms against God and I don't want any part of helping him set up a kingdom that opposes all that is God. This is why Jesus Christ wants us to live as though we are not of the world because friendship with the world is enmity with God.

> Ye adulterers and adulteresses, know ye not that the friendship of the world is enmity with God? whosoever therefore will be a friend of the world is the enemy of God.
>
> James 4:4 (KJV)

In fact, if we examine Scripture, particularly the New Testament, we don't see any prophets, apostles, preachers, or Christians taking up arms to defend themselves or preparing for war because they realize that God did not call us for war. In fact, he calls us and trains and equips us to go into the world and preach and teach the gospel and then baptize those who believe in the name, thereby escaping the rudiment of this world, escaping wars and rumors of wars. In fact, we see the prophets, apostles, disciple, and Christians being so hated for their love for Jesus Christ that they were martyred and persecuted. In fact, we see that they refused to bear arms and that they fled from city to city. Through it all, God did not want them to bear any arms to defend themselves or to repay evil for evil. Rather, we repay evil with love; besides, it is not their fight, for the battle is the Lord's.

> And he said, "Hearken ye, all Judah, and ye inhabitants of Jerusalem, and thou King Jehoshaphat. Thus, saith the Lord unto you, 'Be not afraid nor dismayed by reason of this great multitude; for the battle is not yours, but God's.'"
>
> 2 Chronicles 20:15 (KJV)

> "Recompense to no man evil for evil. Provide things honestly in the sight of all men. If it be possible, as much as lieth in you, live peaceably with all men. Dearly beloved, avenge not yourselves, but rather give place unto wrath: for it is written, vengeance is mine; I will repay," saith the Lord.
>
> Roman 12:17-21 (KJV)

Under the dispensation of grace, Jesus Christ is the spiritual King that governs his people, particularly the body of Christ (Church), or the Christians. Under this dispensation, he has left us a specific model that we are supposed to follow which simply is to love our enemy, love those that hate us and do good to them that spitefully use us. Jesus Christ is the King that governs the righteous church through the ministries of the Holy Spirit, guiding and leading us into all truth. The kingdom of Christ is neither black nor white, Jewish, Greek, nor gentile, but it is composed of a body of individual believers from all walks of life, cultures, and nationalities who have simply accepted Jesus Christ as Lord and Savior and are seeking to live like him. Therefore, there is no particular denomination or religious organization that could claim that their religion or denomination is the only way, as long as it adheres to the strict, doctrinal teaching of Jesus Christ.

MARK OF THE BEAST

UNVEILING THE MARK OF THE BEAST

What is the mark of the beast? Who is this mark of the beast? Is the mark of the beast a system created by an anti-god government. A government influenced by Satan and his demons who are seeking total control of all of mankind economically, financially and spiritually? Or is the mark of the beast the spiritual seed of wicked people who seek or walk in the lust of their father the devil, thereby promoting and establishing an anti-god earth for the glory and honor of their father the devil. In this anti-god government system, it is stated that those who are not in agreement with such satanic kingdoms will have a difficult time surviving. In fact, the only way one could survive in such a kingdom is to join their cause because you can't defeat them. Like the old saying goes, if you can't beat them, join them, or you will have to hide out until the evil forces find you. Once you become a part of this system through your willful acceptance of the mark on you right hand or your forehead, you become one who labors or has full knowledge of Satan and his anti-agendas toward God. Therefore, the mark on the right hand represents your labor, meaning you will be working for this anti-god kingdom and the mark on your forehead represents your knowledge of Satan and its practices and application of satanic knowledge. Therefore, the marks of the beast are those who willfully or forcefully accept Satan's deceptions through obedience to the knowledge of Satan (mark on the forehead) and colabor with Satan (mark on the hands) for the advancement and implementation of slavish institutions of God's chosen people through an anti-god government by teaching, training, and instructing others in the name of Satan.

> Now the Spirit speaketh expressly, that in the latter times some shall depart from the faith, giving heed to seducing spirits, and doctrines of devils; speaking lies in hypocrisy; having their conscience seared with a hot iron…
>
> 1 Timothy 4:1-2 (KJV)

These are the ones who will automatically become agents or slaves to Satan and his demons. Through their works and knowledge, they will institute a satanic government or kingdom, thereby controlling what we buy and sell. In fact, Scripture goes on to say there will be believers who will not be able to bear this system of control and because of hunger and thirst, will try to save their life by giving in to the pressure of this satanic system.

> And he causeth all, both small and great, rich and poor, free and bond, to receive a mark in their right hand, or in their foreheads: And that no man might buy or sell, save he that had the mark, or the name of the beast, or the number of his name. Here is wisdom. Let him that hat understanding count the number of the beast: for it is the number of a man; and his number is Six hundred threescore and six
>
> Revelation 13:16-18 (KJV)

> Whosoever shall seek to save his life shall lose it; and whosoever shall lose his life shall preserve it.
>
> Luke 17:33 (KJV)

So one can imagine how difficult it will be for God's chosen people, the believers of Jesus Christ to refuse to be numbered or branded like a cattle by rejecting the mark of the beast. Those who refuse to receive the mark or to be a part of this satanic system will either die of hunger, torment, or persecution and will eventually be killed for their continual resistance of this new world order or satanic kingdom. In order for us to understand the mark of the beast, we must understand what Scripture teaches and says about

1) What is a beast? and 2) What is a mark? Scripture teaches that a beast is an earthly king with a kingdom, or a political power or figure that controls or influences the masses of people.

> Daniel spake and said, I saw in my vision by night, and, behold, the four winds of the heaven strove upon the great sea. And four great beasts came up from the sea, diverse one from another. The first was like a lion, and had eagle's wings: I beheld till the wings thereof were plucked, and it was lifted up from the earth, and made stand upon the feet as a man, and a man's heart was given to it. And behold another beast, a second, like to a bear, and it raised up itself on one side, and it had three ribs in the mouth of it between the teeth of it: and they said thus unto it, Arise, devour much flesh. After this I beheld, and lo another, like a leopard, which had upon the back of it four wings of a fowl; the beast had also four heads; and dominion was given to it. After this I saw in the night visions, and behold a fourth beast, dreadful and terrible, and strong exceedingly; and it had great iron teeth: it devoured and brake in pieces, and stamped the residue with the feet of it: and it was diverse from all the beasts that were before it; and it had ten horns.
> These great beasts, which are four, are four kings, which shall arise out of the earth.
> Thus he said, The fourth beast shall be the fourth kingdom upon earth, which shall be diverse from all kingdoms, and shall devour the whole earth, and shall tread it down, and break it in pieces.
>
> Daniel 7: 2-7, 17, 23 (KJV)

Now that we have discovered what scriptures teach about what a beast is, let us go on to find out what Scripture also teaches about what a mark is. A mark, throughout Scripture, is always a person, a group of people, or a nation that is set apart, chosen, or sealed by God for his purpose. So, if you are not chosen or selected by God, it means he has rejected you by reason of your disobedience to him, as was evident when God put a mark on Cain. God's rejections are always based on our disobedience to him. When people are disobedient to God, they will be obedient to Satan which will result in the mark of Satan. Therefore, the mark of the beast is when people are marked by an earthly king who is influence by the devil. They have an unwillingness to be submitted to God/Jesus; therefore, they are the children of disobedience and are of the devil because he has chosen them for his purpose or agenda. His purpose or agenda is to unite mankind and lead them to fight his war against God. So, as we examine Scripture, we will discover that the mark of the beast are all those whose names are not written in the Book of Life, those who have willfully accepted Satan's deception of world government, and are laboring and teaching the coming of this satanic government, knowingly or unknowingly. Therefore, we discover what the mark of the beast is by understanding who God's chosen people are in comparison to Satan's chosen people. These chosen people will seek to advance, promote and manifest their God or god's characteristics, as was evident when Jesus Christ told the scribes and Pharisees that they are of their father, the devil, and they will operate in his lusts.

> Why do ye not understand my speech? Even because ye cannot hear my word. Ye are of your father, the devil, and the lusts of your father ye will do. He was a murderer from the beginning, and abode not in the truth, because there is no truth in him. When he speaketh a lie, he speaketh of his own: for he is a liar, and the father of it. And because I tell you the truth, ye believe me not.
>
> John 8:43-45 (KJV)

Let us comb through scriptures and highlight various examples of how God marks his chosen people and see how those who are not marked by God are indirectly chosen by Satan. But before we do that, I want to bring your attention to these three words:

A. *Spiritual seed* – Seed of God or seed of the devil

B. *Physical fruits from this seed* – The manifestation and characteristics of this spiritual seed

C. *Circumcision* – The covenant God made with his chosen people

THE SECOND CURSE

Spiritual seed pertains to what seed you were begotten by the seed of God or the seed of the devil. Are you a child of God (the children light) or a child of the devil (the children of darkness or world)? Physical fruit is the result of the seed; when it's fully grown, it bears forth fruits which are the physical manifestation of one's actions or behavior which are rooted in one's knowledge. This principle is true in determining the mark of the beast. Is your spirit marked by God or marked by the devil? Let us apply this principle to Cain, the first son of Adam and Eve. First, the spiritual seed:

> Whosoever is born of God doth not commit sin; for his seed remaineth in him: and he cannot sin, because he is born of God. In this the children of God are manifest, and the children of the devil: whosoever doeth not righteousness is not of God, neither he that loveth not his brother.
>
> 1 John 3:9-12 (KJV)

Second, physical fruits: Because of Cain's behavior or actions resulting from the seed of the wicked one, he was marked by God; indirectly being marked by Satan, condemned, confined, and isolated from the rest of humanity to a specific location resulting in the second curse. As the first curse caused mankind to be removed from the presence of God, the second curse is the removal of wicked man from the presence of mankind or humanity. Here is scriptural proof, the example of Cain being marked and then isolated from the rest of the world which is the second curse God place upon mankind that walks in disobedience.

> "Behold, thou hast driven me out this day from the face of the earth; and from thy face shall I be hid; and I shall be a fugitive and a vagabond in the earth; and it shall come to pass, that every one that findeth me shall slay me."
>
> Genesis 4:14-15 (KJV)

> "I have sinned; what shall I do unto thee, O thou preserver of men? Why hast thou set me as a mark against thee, so that I am a burden to myself?"
>
> Job 7:20 (KJV)

Therefore a mark, throughout Scripture, has to do with those who God has accepted or rejected by reasons of obedience or disobedience to him and his laws. What is the implanted seed of those who walk and live in the spirit of God or are influence by spirit of the devil? Walking or living in the spirit produces the fruits of the spirit which are love, joy, peace, long suffering, kindness, goodness, faithfulness, gentleness, etc., which come out of our characters. Is your character which leads to your behavior, uniting and promoting godly characteristics or is it dividing and producing ungodly characteristics that violate God's laws? Are you walking in love and in accordance with your lifestyle through the teachings of Jesus Christ? This was the only request he asked of us who trusted and believed in his name before his ascension, commissioning us to teach and baptize in his name. This request brings total freedoms for those who are in bondage to Satan and his demons. Or are you walking in hate and teaching a gospel that is contrary to the teachings of Jesus Christ and that promotes satanic agendas that lead to the enslaving God's people, the Christians?

THE MARK OF CIRCUMCISION

Circumcision is another way God marks his chosen people from the rest of the world. Under the dispensation of the Law, God's chosen people were marked through circumcision. God made a covenant with his people by having them circumcise every male that was born in their house. God chose Abraham to be the one who would be the father of his covenant people. He told Abraham to circumcise himself and all males born thereafter in his household as a mark or a sign between him and Abraham.

> And I will make my covenant between me and thee, and will multiply thee exceedingly. And Abram fell on his face: and God talked with him, saying…
>
> Genesis 17: 2-5 (KJV)

This covenant was the beginning of a sign of how God begins to mark a people and chose them and their posterity to be his chosen people. Abraham entered into a covenant relationship with God; as a result of choosing him, God promised to be his protector, provider, and comforter. The purpose of this covenant was for God to train and instruct a people chosen by Him concerning Him, teaching them His love, His laws, and His holiness and to eventually incarnate Himself in the form of Jesus Christ as Emmanuel, God among his people; thus, his promise could be fulfilled to Abraham when he said those that those who bless him He will bless, and those who curse him, He will curse.

GOD MARKS HIS PEOPLE CORPORATELY

Let me also reveal how scriptures demonstrate how God marks his people corporately by separating them from the world from the children of darkness. Scriptures demonstrate that God marks his people not only through spiritual seed or circumcision but by setting them apart from all other people all those who do not have knowledge of God. A familiar scripture that comes into mind is when we see how God corporately marked his people, the children of Israel while they were in bondage, slaves to the Egyptians. The Egyptians also indirectly marked their people by privileging them to be masters and rulers over God's people, all those whose ethnicity was not of Egypt. The Egyptians at that time were the most powerful country in the world. They began to enslave the children of Israel, God's chosen people; God's people cried out to Him for over four hundred years. God finally decided to hear their cries and came to their rescue and sought out a man to go set them free; thus, God commissioned Moses to go tell the pharaoh to "Let my people go." The pharaoh said, "Who is the Lord that I may obey his voice?" (Exodus 5:1-2, KJV) Moses' request from Pharaoh established the conditions of the Hebrew slaves much harder; now they were expected to make bricks without straw. Isn't this always the case? When God is getting ready to free you from the grip of the enemy, the enemy begins to put more pressure or intensify his assaults toward you. But I want to encourage you to know and be assured that it is God who will fight the enemy for you. So the enemy can increase his pressure on us all he wants; he will be fighting against God and we know who will win. God told Moses to go tell Pharaoh a second time to let his people go so they could come and worship him in the wilderness and that if he refused he would bring about a plague upon Egypt. God said to Moses, "Pharaoh will ask for a sign." Why would Pharaoh ask for a sign? In that way, he could try to determine where his power was coming from. This reminds me of the scribes and Pharisees asking Jesus to show them a sign. This is how Jesus replied:

> Then certain of the scribes and of the Pharisees answered, saying, Master, we would see a sign from thee. But he answered and said unto them, An evil and adulterous generation seeketh after a sign; and there shall no sign be given to it, but the sign of the prophet Jonas: For as Jonas was three days and three nights in the whale's belly; so shall the Son of man be three days and three nights in the heart of the earth.
>
> Mathew 12:38-40 (KJV)

Moses did what God told him to do and showed Pharaoh a miracle which showed that Moses meant business and that a higher power was backing him. And Aaron, through Moses's instruction, threw the rod down and it turned into a serpent; Pharaoh's magicians also threw their rods on the ground and they turned into serpents but God's serpent swallowed the magicians' serpents.

> And the LORD spake unto Moses and unto Aaron, saying, When Pharaoh shall speak unto you, saying, Shew a miracle for you: then thou shalt say unto Aaron, Take thy rod, and cast it before Pharaoh, and it shall become a serpent. And Moses and Aaron went in unto Pharaoh, and they did so as the LORD had commanded: and Aaron cast down his rod before Pharaoh, and before his servants, and it became a serpent. Then Pharaoh also called the wise men and the sorcerers: now the magicians of Egypt, they also did in like manner with their enchantments.
>
> Exodus 7:8-11 (KJV)

This miracle did not impress Pharaoh because they were able to duplicate that miracle. In essence, Pharaoh told Moses, "If your God wants to deliver his people out my hands, he has to come up with something better than this." This was Moses's and Aaron's first miracle and God began to destroy Egypt with ten plagues. God told Moses to instruct Pharaoh to let his people go so they could worship him. But God told Moses that he would harden Pharaoh's heart so that he would not let them go. But why would God do that, harden Pharaoh's heart so that he would refuse to let his people go? Because through Pharaoh's refusal, God could show all his powers over the Egyptians by destroying the most powerful government on earth and by letting them know that there is no one like Him in all the earth or in the heavens, for He alone is God. Secondly, to show that God could do with us whatever he wants especially with kings, queens, presidents, etc., that it is by him and him alone they exist and reign. This is why God said to Pharaoh that it was for this reason he raised him up. Everyone born into this world with the breath of life is in God's hands. In this case, God was making Pharaoh a stubborn king so that he could demonstrate all his power over the Egyptians' kingdom, thereby destroying the Egyptians' kingdom and dismantling all their false gods and idol worships.

THE FIRST PLAGUE – WATER TO BLOOD

The first plague was turning the waters into blood which did not impress Pharaoh and his magicians because they were able to do the same thing.

> And the LORD spake unto Moses, Say unto Aaron, Take thy rod and stretch out thine hand upon the waters of Egypt upon their streams, upon their rivers and upon their ponds, upon all their pools of water that they may become

blood; and that there may be blood throughout all the land of Egypt, both in vessels of wood and in vessels of stone.

And Moses and Aaron did so, as the LORD commanded; and he lifted up the rod, and smote the waters that were in the river, in sight of Pharaoh and in the sight of his servants; and all the waters that were in the river were turned to blood.

And the fish that was in the river died, and the river stank, and the Egyptians could not drink of the water of the river; and there was blood throughout all the land of Egypt.

And the magicians of Egypt did so with their enchantments: and Pharaoh's heart was hardened, neither did he hearken unto them; as the Lord had said.

Exodus 7:19-22 (KJV)

THE SECOND PLAGUE – FROGS

The second plague brought frogs upon the land of Egypt that went within their houses, bed chambers, etc. Pharaoh's magicians, through enchantment and sorcery were able to also perform the same thing. So again, Pharaoh was not impressed, not knowing that God was just hardening his heart.

> And the LORD spake unto Moses, Say unto Aaron, Stretch forth thine hand with thy rod over the streams, over the rivers, and over the ponds, and cause frogs to come up upon the land of Egypt. And Aaron stretched out his hand over the waters of Egypt; and the frogs came up, and covered the land of Egypt. And the magicians did so with their enchantments, and brought up frogs upon the land of Egypt. Then Pharaoh called for Moses and Aaron, and said, intreat the LORD, that he may take

away the frogs from me, and from my people; and I will let the people go, that they may do sacrifice unto the LORD.

Exodus 8:5-8 (KJV)

THE THIRD PLAGUE – GNATS OR LICE

The third plague was when God brought lice throughout the land of Egypt from the dust of the earth. Again, Pharaoh's magicians through their enchantment tried to bring lice but they could not do it and they told Pharaoh it was the finger of God; this got their attention.

> And the LORD said unto Moses, Say unto Aaron, Stretch out thy rod, and smite the dust of the land, tht it may become lice throughout all the land of Egypt. And they did so, for Aaron stretched out his hand with his rod, and smote the dust of the earth, and it became lice in man, and in beast, all the dust of the land became lice throughout all the land of Egypt. And the magicians did so with their enchantments to bring forth lice, but they could not; so there were lice upon man, and upon beast. Then the magicians said unto Pharaoh, "This is the finger of God," and Pharaoh's heart was hardened, and he hearkened not unto them; as the Lord had said.
>
> Exodus 8:16-19 (KJV)

THE FOURTH PLAGUE – FLIES

From the fourth plague on, God begins to mark his chosen people by making a clear distinction between his people and the Egyptians. In this plague, God promised that no swarm of flies would go to the land of Goshen where his chosen people were.

And the LORD said unto Moses, Rise up early in the morning, and stand before Pharaoh; lo, he cometh forth to the water; and say unto him, Thus saith the LORD, Let my people go, that they may serve me.

Else, if thou wilt not let my people go, behold, I will send swarms of flies upon thee, and upon thy servants, and upon thy people, and into thy houses; and the houses of the Egyptians shall be full of swarms of flies, and also the ground whereon they are.

And I will sever in that day the land of Goshen, in which my people dwell, that no swarms of flies shall be there; to the end thou mayest know that I am the LORD in the midst of the earth.

And I will put a division between my people and they people; to morrow shall this sign be.

And the LORD did so; and there came a grievous swarm of flies into the house of Pharaoh, and into his servants' houses, and into the land of Egypt: the land was corrupted by reason of the swarm of flies.

And Pharaoh called for Moses and for Aaron, and said, Go ye, sacrifice to your God in the land.

Exodus 8:20-25 (KJV)

THE FIFTH PLAGUE
LIVESTOCK DISEASE

God again distinguished his chosen people. In this fifth plague, God marked the children of Israel and made sure none of their livestock was killed by this next plague. Pharaoh sent his people to go and see if any of the children of Israel's cattle had died and to his disbelief, it was confirmed that none of God's chosen people's cattle had died.

Then the LORD said unto Moses, go in unto Pharaoh, and tell him, Thus saith the LORD God of the Hebrews, Let my people go, that they may serve me.

For if thou refuse to let them go, and will hold them still.

Behold, the hand of the LORD is upon they cattle which is in the field, upon the horses, upon the asses, upon the camels, upon the oxen, and upon the sheep: there shall be a very grievous murrain.

And the LORD shall sever between the cattle of Israel and the cattle of Egypt: and there shall nothing die of all that is the children's of Israel.

And the LORD appointed a set time, saying, To morrow the LORD shall do this thing in the land.

And the LORD did that thing on the morrow, and all the cattle of Egypt died: but the cattle of the children of Israel died not one.

And Pharaoh sent, and behold, there was not one of the cattle of the Israelites dead. And the heart of Pharaoh was hardened, and he did not let the people go.

Exodus 9:1-7 (KJV)

THE SIXTH PLAGUE – BOILS

And the LORD said unto Moses and unto Aaron, take to you handfuls of ashes of the furnace, and let Moses sprinkle it toward the heaven in the sight of Pharaoh. And it shall become small dust in all the land of Egypt, and shall be a boil breaking forth with blains upon man, and upon beast, throughout all the land of Egypt. And they took ashes of the furnace, and stood before Pharaoh; and Moses sprinkled it up toward heaven; and it became a boil breaking forth with blains upon man, and upon beast. And the magicians could not stand before Moses because of the boils; for the boil was upon the magicians, and upon all the Egyptians. And the LORD hardened the heart of Pharaoh, and he hearkened not unto them; as the LORD had spoken unto Moses.

Exodus 9:8-12 (KJV)

THE SEVENTH PLAGUE THUNDER AND HAIL

With this next plague, God again marked his people by distinguishing them from the Egyptians. He rained down hail from heaven and made sure that no hail touched the land of Goshen where his chosen or marked people lived. God rained down hail from the sky that destroyed man, beast, and castles that were in the field; all those who did not regard his word died.

> And the LORD said unto Moses, Rise up early in the morning, and stand before Pharaoh, and say unto him, Thus saith the LORD God of the Hebrews, Let my people go, that they may serve me. For I will at this time send all my plagues upon thine heart, and upon thy servants, and upon thy people; that thou mayest know that there is none like me in all the earth. For now, I will stretch out my hand, that I may smite thee and thy people with pestilence; and thou shalt be cut off from the earth. And in very deed for this cause have I raised thee up, for to shew in thee my power; and that my name may be declared throughout all the earth. As yet exaltest thou thyself against my people, that thou wilt not let them go? Behold, tomorrow about this time I will cause it to rain a very grievous hail, such as hath not been in Egypt since the foundation thereof even until now. Send therefore now, and gather thy cattle, and all that thou hast in the field; for upon every man and beast which shall be found in the field, and shall not be brought home, the hail shall come down upon them, and they shall die. He that feared the word of the LORD among the

servants of Pharaoh made his servants and his cattle flee into the houses: And he that regarded not the word of the LORD left his servants and his cattle in the field. And the LORD said unto Moses, stretch forth thine hand toward heaven, that there may be hail in all the land of Egypt, upon man, and upon beast, and upon every herb of the field, throughout the land of Egypt. And Moses stretched forth his rod toward heaven: and the LORD sent thunder and hail, and the fire ran along upon the ground; and the LORD rained hail upon the land of Egypt. So, there was hail, and fire mingled with the hail, very grievous, such as there was none like it in all the land of Egypt since it became a nation. And the hail smote throughout all the land of Egypt all that was in the field, both man and beast; and the hail smote every herb of the field, and brake every tree of the field. Only in the land of Goshen, where the children of Israel were, was there no hail.

Exodus 9:13-26 (KJV)

THE EIGHTH PLAGUE – LOCUSTS

God, taunting and tormenting the Egyptians brought about another plague, locusts which devoured all herbs the hail did not destroy. At this time, the Egyptian servants were begging Pharaoh to let God's people go so that they could go worship him in the wilderness. The reason I said God was taunting and tormenting the Egyptians is because He could have killed and wiped out the whole of the Egyptians in a second just with a stroke of his fingers, if he wanted to.

> "Else, if thou refuse to let my people go, behold, to morrow will I bring the locusts into thy coast: And they shall cover the face of the earth, that one cannot be able to see the earth: and they shall eat the residue of that which is escaped, which remaineth unto you from the

hail, and shall eat every tree which groweth for you out of the field: And they shall fill thy houses, and the houses of all thy servants, and the houses of all the Egyptians; which neither thy fathers, nor thy fathers' fathers have seen, since the day that they were upon the earth unto this day. And he turned himself, and went out from Pharaoh. And Pharaoh's servants said unto him, How long shall this man be a snare unto us? let the men go, that they may serve the LORD their God: knowest thou not yet that Egypt is destroyed? And Moses and Aaron were brought again unto Pharaoh: and he said unto them, Go, serve the LORD your God: but who are they that shall go? And Moses said, We will go with our young and with our old, with our sons and with our daughters, with our flocks and with our herds will we go; for we must hold a feast unto the LORD. And he said unto them, Let the LORD be so with you, as I will let you go, and your little ones: look to it; for evil is before you. Not so: go now ye that are men, and serve the LORD; for that ye did desire. And they were driven out from Pharaoh's presence. And the LORD said unto Moses, Stretch out thine hand over the land of Egypt for the locusts, that they may come up upon the land of Egypt, and eat every herb of the land, even all that the hail hath left. And Moses stretched forth his rod over the land of Egypt, and the LORD brought an east wind upon the land all that day, and all that night; and when it was morning, the east wind brought the locusts. And the locust went up over all the land of Egypt, and rested in all the coasts of Egypt: very grievous were they; before them there were no such locusts as they, neither after them shall be such. For they covered the face of the whole earth, so that the land was darkened; and they did eat every herb of the land, and all the fruit of the trees which the hail had left: and there remained not any green thing in the trees, or in the herbs of the field, through all the land of Egypt".

Exodus 10:4-15 (KJV)

THE NINTH PLAGUE – DARKNESS

God again marked his people by distinguishing between them and the Egyptians that no darkness would come upon the land where his chosen people dwell, while all the Egyptians would not have light.

> They saw not one another, neither rose any from his place for three days: but all the children of Israel had light in their dwellings.
>
> Exodus 10:21-23 (KJV)

THE TENTH PLAGUE DEATH OF THE FIRSTBORN

And the Lord said unto Moses, "Yet will I bring one plague more upon Pharaoh, and upon Egypt; afterwards he will let you go hence: when he shall let you go, he shall surely thrust you out hence altogether. Speak now in the ears of the people, and let every man borrows of his neighbor, and every woman of her neighbor, jewels of silver and jewels of gold. And the LORD gave the people favour in the sight of the Egyptians. Moreover, the man Moses was very great in the land of Egypt, in the sight of Pharaoh's servants, and in the sight of the people. And Moses said, thus saith the LORD, About midnight will I go out into the midst of Egypt: And all the firstborn in the land of Egypt shall die, from the first born of Pharaoh that sitteth upon his throne, even unto the firstborn of the maidservant that is behind the mill; and all the firstborn of beasts. And there shall be a great cry throughout all the land of Egypt, such as there was none like it, nor shall be like it any more. But against any of the children of Israel shall not a dog move his tongue, against man or beast: that ye may know how that the LORD doth put a difference between the Egyptians and Israel.

Exodus 11:1-7 (KJV)

Again, God marked his people by making sure none of his chosen people's firstborn died, only the Egyptians'.

Understanding the ten plagues God released upon the Egyptians brings a certain comfort to us Christians because we understand that through the plagues, he preserved his chosen people and did not destroy his people with the Egyptians, just as He told Abraham when he was interceding for Lot, his nephew, that he would not destroy the righteous with the wicked. Likewise, the plague which is soon coming upon the world will destroy all those who do not believe in Jesus Christ. God will preserve those he has marked because we are his chosen people who believe in his only begotten son. Therefore, no evil shall befall us nor shall any plagues come near our dwelling.

> A thousand shall fall at thy side, and ten thousand at thy right hand; but it shall not come nigh thee. Only with thine eyes shalt thou behold and see the reward of the wicked. A thousand shall fall at thy side, and ten thousand at thy right hand; but it shall not come nigh thee. Only with thine eyes shalt thou behold and see the reward of the wicked. Because thou hast made the LORD, which is my refuge, even the most high, thy habitation; There shall no evil befall thee, neither shall any plague come nigh thy dwelling.

Psalm 91:7-10 (KJV)

Under the dispensation of grace, God's chosen people are all those who have accepted his holy and only begotten Son, Jesus Christ, as Lord and Savior. God annulled his previous methods by which he marked his chosen people because they were temporary; a foreshadow of things to come until the real and permanent way was established which is Jesus Christ. Therefore, those who confess Jesus Christ as Lord and Savior are God's sons and daughters, his chosen people. It is through Jesus Christ that God marks his chosen people. Below are three ways that God marks his people under the dispensation of grace:

> A. Spiritual seed of Jesus Christ–Those who by obedience have accepted Jesus Christ as Lord and Savior are set apart and chosen by God (John 3:16).
> B. Spiritual circumcision is the heart of circumcision, which is the cutting or taking away of the heart of stone and replacing it with the heart of flesh so that God can put his spirit within us.

> "A new heart also will I give you, and a new spirit will I put within you: and I will take away the stony heart out of your flesh, and I will give you a heart of flesh."

> Ezekiel 36:26-27 (KJV)

> For circumcision verily profiteth, if thou keep the law: but if thou be a breaker of the law, thy circumcision is made uncircumcision. Therefore, if the uncircumcision keep the righteousness of the law, shall not his uncircumcision be counted for circumcision?

> Roman 2:25-29 (KJV)

> C. God corporately marks his people by giving then a new name, calling us Christians, denoting a new relationship or newness of life; just as he did with Abram when he established his covenant with him and changed his name from Abram to Abraham. This relationship that God calls the believers or Christians is based on five principles that will guarantee the successfulness of every believer that applies these principles.

1. Faith in God/Jesus Christ – One must believe in Jesus Christ as Lord and Savior to have faith in God.
2. Obedience to God's Word or voice – One must be obedient to the totality of God's Word, because obedience it is the only way we demonstrate that we love God and seek to apply it to our daily life.
3. **Humility** – One must humble themselves before God and God will exalt them, for Scripture says that God hates a prideful heart.
4. Integrity – One must walk in integrity so that we don't make a mockery of or shame God's name.
5. Love – One must seek to love all of mankind, black, white, yellow, or red and do good to them, not rendering evil for evil but rather, loving our enemies and praying for those who hate us. God has no calls to war; while the world walks in war, God wants his chosen people to walk in love.

These five principles mark and separate Christians the world. The opposite of these five principles distinguish the children of the devil, including those who walk in darkness. These children are marked or chosen by the devil, so they likewise display the characteristics of the devil, which are: 1) Faith in the devil or self, 2) Disobedience to God's Word or voice but obedience to the devil and his demons 3) Pride, 4) Dishonesty or lacking integrity, and 5) Walking in hate, or hateful.

Therefore, the mark of the beast is the willful acceptance of the devil's deceptions by the people. This movement toward a one world government through the spread of democracy, is the hope of uniting all kings and kingdoms under the leadership of Satan, the son of perdition to war against the second coming of Jesus Christ. Once this objective is achieved, they will then seek to root all Christians out of this world which will be the greatest persecution ever seen upon God's chosen people (modernday Christians).

ARMAGEDDON

GOD KNOWS US BY NAME, THE DEVIL BY NUMBER

The great persecution of God's people (Christians) will be in the up and coming century. This is distinguished by those Christians who refuse to accept or take the mark of the beast. This mark identifies you as a child of the devil; therefore, whoever is a child of God will refuse being marked. In the twenty-first century, new understanding has emerged as to what this mark of the beast is. This understanding simply incorporates our technological advancements in biochips to Scripture by applying scriptures like "He caused great, big, small, free, bond to take the mark of the beast, and those without the mark cannot buy or sell anything (Revelation 13:16-17 KJV). This is a clear indication of total global control over all humans' affairs. What then is this mark of the beast in the twenty-first century? Is the mark of the beast a biochip Satan seeks to implant on the right hand or forehead of everyone who is living during the great tribulation? Is this the means by which he achieves his method of controlling all of mankind, through dictating what one can buy or what one can sell? All those who do not have this biochip or mark will not be able to function in this world. What is this biochip? This biochip is a micro chip, small like a grain of rice inserted under the human skin for identification and tracking purposes. This biochip will contain all your personal information from inception to the day you die. It will contain medical records, social security numbers, schooling, work history, criminal history and travel logs like passports, etc., for the purpose of monitoring your every movement. The primary motive behind such invasion of privacy and the need to monitor civilians is Satan's ignorance and since he desires to be like God, he thinks by monitoring you and I; it will make him all knowing because he will know where you are at all times. However, he has managed to influence mankind that it is for their safety. The excuse he uses to advance this agenda is fear—the fear of terrorist activities, kidnapping of children and babies, car theft, crimes, murder, etc. It seems like a logical solution to implement a concept that people will be willing to forfeit their privacy in exchange for safety. Such manipulation of the human leads to the technological slavery of the human race of the twenty-first century or the up and coming century. So the trick or deception is to assault the world by creating chaos, chaos, chaos, till the people or the world will be willing to accept any form of monitoring system that will attempt to guarantee your safety for you and your loved ones. As a result, we see the proliferation of global wars, nuclear showdowns, economic woes, increases in natural disasters, and ungodliness as the workers and the instructors of these global agendas forcefully or willfully surrender us to a satanic order. The hatred of these demonic forces make up the inhumane activities that will go on in this satanic world order. They impose their will upon the human race as they get their revenge against God for kicking them out of heaven. Jesus Christ is the only God that truly loves the human race and he proved that by sacrificing his life for us. In fact, the devil and his demonic forces will lead mankind into a great slaughter in the battle of Armageddon against God. God doesn't need any monitoring devices or chips to know where we are or what we are doing, for he knows our thoughts and sees everything that we do. This is the same deception Satan told Eve that if she eats of this forbidden fruit, she will be like God. Adam and Eve never desired to be God, for they were already in the image of God. It is Satan who desires to be like God. Satan desires to know where you at all times, for he thinks that will make him all knowing. He can fool man with his deceptions and his tricks but he cannot fool God and his chosen people, the Christians. This reminds me of prisoners who are incarcerated; the prison guards need to know where their prisoner is at all times. In order for him to know where you are, he has to number you and constantly keep count of you by tracking your every movement. This is the mass institution of slavery and ignorant men, particularly leaders are falling for this global satanic deception. Jesus cautioned us to leave these blind leaders alone when he told us if the blind lead the blind, both will fall into a ditch (Matthew 15:14, KJV). God knows us by name because he was the one who created us. God knowledge of us and our names denotes the personal relationship he has with everyone who has confessed his only and holy Son as Lord and Savior. Satan is not seeking to establish a relationship with those who ignorantly believe in him because he has no love for them. After he uses them, he discards them and leaves them abandoned, alone to fend for themselves on the Day of Judgment before Jesus Christ. He does not care about them, nor does he have a father's heart because he did not create them. Therefore, he seeks to implant everyone whose name is not written in the Book of Life by setting up a technological system that will enable him to number you, just like they number all those who are incarcerated. This will enabled Satan to achieve his long-awaited agenda to unite with mankind for the purpose of leading them into a global war against the beloved Son of God, Jesus Christ, the Creator of heaven and earth. The implementation of this biochip will allow him to achieve his means of controlling all of mankind, economically, financially, and spiritually: economically, by prohibiting and controlling the use of our resources; financially, by controlling and managing our funds which they can freeze at will or use as they eidh because they will be in slavery institutions; and spiritually, as they will hinder and persecute all those who believe in Jesus Christ by tempting them to renounce Jesus Christ as Lord and Savior. The implementation of this biochip will be possible through technology to maintain control and prohibit anyone without the biochip to buy or sell anything. The new world order will force people into forced labor, eventually enslaving them, depriving them of any rights or benefits due to anyone who is an citizen. These oppressions and depressions will create a degenerated people who no longer will know who their God is. Therefore, another understanding of the mark of the beast is a biochip that Satan, the adversary, uses to number all people, some accepting it willfully and others by force as they prepare the world for an all-out war against the Creator of heaven and earth. And will this biochip cause believers of Jesus Christ to renounce their Lord and Savior if they are forcefully implanted? Or is the mark of the beast the fruits of the spiritual seed of the devil, as outlined at the beginning of this chapter? Or is the mark of the beast and the number of his name the total of the six hundred and sixty-sixth king of the earth? And this king is going to number his people and prepare them for the war of Armageddon, just like any commander who counts how many soldiers they have before going to war.

> Here is wisdom. Let him that hath understanding count the number of the beast: for it is the number of a man; and his number is six hundred threescore and six.
>
> Revelation 13:18 (KJV)

ARMAGEDDON
(THE LAST WAR OR THE OMEGA WAR)

> And I saw three unclean spirits like frogs come out of the mouth of the dragon, and out of the mouth of the beast, and out of the mouth of the false prophet. For they are the spirits of devils, working miracles, which go forth unto the kings of the earth and of the whole world, to gather them to the battle of that great day of God Almighty.
>
> Revelation 16:13-14 (KJV)

For the past two thousand years, after the resurrection of Jesus Christ, Satan and his demons advanced their kingdom. They are slowly dismantling the unity of the Christian brotherhood through false denominations and false religious organizations that infiltrate Christian churches through cultures, traditions, and philosophies, and through seduction of demonic doctrines, spiritual greed which culminate to lust for power, money, wealth, etc. They have managed to buy out ministers, world leaders, and kings and rewarded them handsomely for the cooperation of the souls of God's people (Christians), through the teaching of false doctrine. Just like the same way Satan tried to buy Jesus's allegiance to him by offering him all the riches of the world. But Jesus turned it down by rebuking him because it all belongs to him, for he created all things, even Satan. And with the coming war, he is going to restore all things back to his rule. These false prophets, teachers, and leaders have received the spirit of frogs to teach God's people false doctrines, persuading all those whose name is not written in the Book of Life by means of the miracles they performed, manipulating and enslaving the heart of man to follow Satan's agendas for a new world order. They will instruct their followers and condition them to accept the false messiah, the coming of the anti-Christ who will sit in the rebuilt temple exalting himself as God.

> Now we beseech you, brethren, by the coming of our Lord Jesus Christ, and by our gathering together unto him, that ye be not soon shaken in mind, or be troubled, neither by spirit, nor by word, nor by letter as from us, as that the day of Christ is at hand. Let no man deceive you by any means: for that day shall not come, except there comes a falling away first, and that man of sin be revealed, the son of perdition; Who opposeth and exalteth himself above all that is called God, or that is worshipped; so that he as God sitteth in the temple of God, shewing himself that he is God.
>
> 2 Thessalonians 2:1-4 (KJV)

Satan's going to sit in the temple, masquerading himself has God? You guessed it—the temple of God in Jerusalem which was not supposed to have been rebuilt for the third time after its destruction which was prophesied by Jesus Christ. This is why Jesus Christ said to his disciples that this temple would be utterly destroyed and not one stone would be left upon it.

> And Jesus went out, and departed from the temple: and his disciples came to him for to shew him the buildings of the temple. And Jesus said unto them, See ye not all these things? verily I say unto you, There shall not be left here one stone upon another, that shall not be thrown down.
>
> Matthew 24:1-2 (KJV)

This prophecy was fulfilled in 70 AD, when the Jews wanted to be freed from the hands of their oppressors, the Roman Empire. This led to a great revolt, the first Jewish-Roman war. The result of this war led to the temple's utter destruction that was so grave that not even one stone was left upon another; this was the second destruction of Solomon's temple. The first destruction of the temple was by the hands of King Nebuchadnezzar. God gave Nebuchadnezzar the authority to war with his chosen people because of their worship to many false gods. Nebuchadnezzar defeated the children of the southern kingdom. The southern kingdom was made of the tribes of Judah and Benjamin. After he defeated them, he took all the prominent people, particularly the children of royalty and all those who were skilled and gifted in arts, science, math etc., and brought them into Babylon as slaves to be used for his kingdom. Daniel, Shadrack, Meshack, and Abednego were among the captives. He left all the sick, poor, and maimed people in Jerusalem. Then he took all the gold precious objects in the temple and brought it to Babylon. The northern kingdom was comprised of the ten tribes of Israel which had already been taken into captivity by the Assyrians, also for their idolatry. God, through his mercy and grace, allowed the temple to be rebuilt in the time of war by the prophet Nehemiah, under the protection of King Darius. The temple was intact when Jesus Christ appeared and he predicted that the temple was going to be destroyed again. The temple was not intended to be rebuild a third time; that's why Jesus said no stone shall be left upon one another (Matthew 23:33-39, KJV). This is why Jesus Christ said to destroy this temple and he will raise it three days (John 2:19, KJV). The rebuilding of the temple is going to be the body of Christ, for Christians are the temple of God.

> Know ye not that ye are the temple of God, and that the Spirit of God dwelleth in you? If any man defiles the temple of God, him shall God destroy; for the temple of God is holy, which temple ye are.
>
> 1 Corinthian 3:16-17 (KJV)

Therefore, the rebuilding of the temple for the third time is for the preparation of the coming of the false messiah, the anti-Christ. Who is going to sit in the temple of God, acting like he is God?

> Who opposeth and exalteth himself above all that is called God, or that is worshiped; so that he as God sitteth in the temple of God, shewing himself that he is God.
>
> 2 Thessalonians 2: 4 (KJV)

He will establish a temporarily peace within the Middle East region and in three and a half years, he will break the peace treaty and will begin to persecute all of God's people; those who believe that Jesus Christ is the Messiah, the only Savior of the world. By his craftiness, he will cause mankind to redefine God's universal law that governed them by setting up his anti-god government, a kingdom by which he is the one who influences the affairs of mankind through a democratic government by letting the people think they have a part or a choice in his kingdom and that government is ruled by the people. This sphere of influence by the enemy is primary in the area of kings, queens, presidents, prime ministers, church leaders, etc.; anyone who has a large following or is able to influence people will receive the spirit of a frog which will go throughout the world deceiving people.

> Little children, it is the last time: and as ye have heard that antichrist shall come, even now are there many antichrists; whereby we know that it is the last time. They went out from us, but they were not of us; for if they had being of us, they would no doubt have continued with us: but they went out, that they might be made manifest that they were not all of us.
>
> 1 John 2:18-19 (KJV)

THE PURPOSE OF THE MAN OF SIN BEING REVEALED

The son of perdition is going to be revealed soon. The primary purpose of his appearance is to lead mankind into Armageddon, the final war when Satan and his demons unite with mankind to war against God. Before the son of perdition is revealed, there must be a certain global, climatic environmental change or shift that allow him and his agents to occupy the earth. In order words, earth will shift into a battleground. The spirit of Satan in the man of sin will not be revealed unless this present world is extremely evil, violent, disorderly and chaotic to the point where there is no sense of right or wrong; this is what we are experiencing today. Satan does not and cannot govern over Christian people; Christian people will constantly remind him of God's laws and righteousness. He will want to corrupt them by making them evil, and if he can't, he will seek to kill them.

The last thing an evil person wants around is a righteous person, going against his wishes. He does not want anyone in his kingdom second guessing him because he does not want what he tried to do in heaven in his attempt to overthrow God to happen in his kingdom. So he is going to make sure he unites all world governments under his leadership. He does not want to fight God and then to worry about fighting other world governments that do not compromise with him. Therefore, he is going to rule over evil spirits and wicked people which will happen because there is no honor among wicked people. These are the ones who the Bible says their names are not written in the Book of Life because they have not accepted Jesus Christ as Lord and Savior because Jesus Christ is the book of life. In retrospect, when the man of sin is revealed, it will be just like Sodom and Gomorrah and the days of Noah, when mankind, under the influence of Satan and his demons did wickedness and their heart were evil continuously causing the wrath of God to come upon them and utterly destroy them.

There are two things that must happen before we consider the ushering in of mankind into the final war of the world, the war of Armageddon. First is the unification of all governments under one world government system called the new world order. This will create the unity of all earthly kings under one leader, the son of perdition. Any nation or government who oppose or fails to comply with this global initiative will be condemned and destroyed. This is why I believe we are living in the time of unrest where there are wars being fought on every corner of the globe; there are famines through the world, earthquakes, hurricanes, revolutions, uprisings, floods, etc. The purpose of these wars is to get rid of all other governments or regimes that will be a potential threat to the establishment of this new world order, and in doing so, they unify all leaders under one umbrella; the democratic government of the world. Democracy will be the last standing government of the world because it incorporates the evil intention of the will of the people to be self-governed.

Democracy will be the primary force under the subtle influence of Satan and his demons as they establish total control over mankind and lead them into the greatest slaughter known to mankind, when mankind seeks to war against their Creator under the deception of Satan and his demons. Scripture says that day will be a great feast for all the birds of the air when they eat the carcasses of kings, queens, captains, etc.

> And I saw an angel standing in the sun; and he cried with a loud voice, saying to all the fowls that fly in the midst of heaven, "Come and gather yourselves together unto the supper of the great God; That ye may eat the flesh of kings, and the flesh of captains, and the flesh of mighty men, and the flesh of horses, and of them that sit on them, and the flesh of all men, both free and bond, both small and great."
>
> Revelation 19:17-19 (KJV)

Democracy is going to continue to expand its territory until the whole world is democratized, thereby making it a kingdom under the full infiltration of Satan and his demons and human agents. There will be no toleration of any other form of independent governments within this anti-god kingdom because they must be united to fight against God/Jesus as he comes to judge all of world. One world government, whereby all the kingdoms of this world are united under one common goal. What is the common goal? This common goal is to fight for their freedom of the sovereign God who judges heaven and earth and to establish a universal democratic system where they choose among themselves who should lead them while welcoming all demonic forces into their world. In order for this global agenda to be implemented and be successful, he has to have full cooperation from all people and their respective governments. The second thing that must happen before we consider the ushering in of mankind's entrance into the final war, the war of the world; Armageddon, is the unification of all people under the subtle influence of Satan and his demons through the governments. Any citizens or civilians that do not comply with these global agendas will be tortured and killed. The common goal of the uniting of kings and their people under the institution of one world government or kingdom is for the preparation and the revealing of the son of perdition, or the man of sin.

> Let no man deceive you by any means: for that day shall not come, except there come a falling away first, and that man of sin be revealed, the son of perdition; Who opposeth and exalteth himself above all that is called God, or that is worshipped; so that he as God sitteth in the temple of God, shewing himself that he is God.
>
> 2 Thessalonians 2:3-7 (KJV)

Satan's people are human agents who are working tirelessly to make earth an environment where Satan and his demons will be able to dwell; the kind of environment conducive for these fallen beings; an environment where good is evil and evil is good; an environment where unrighteousness is the norm, where greed and power are the thirst and hunger of evil men, where love is rooted in lust.

After the son of sin has been revealed and has gathered the world army in unity under a democratic government, there shall be a greater wonder in the skies. Scripture says every eye shall see him. Jesus will appear in the skies and everyone living will see him. He is coming with ten thousand of his angels to war against the rebellion of his creation; Satan, his demons and mankind who have been deceived and have joined the beast (earthly king) to fight against God, the Creator of heaven and earth. This is where all those who have been briefed will take their position. World government officials, world armies, and all citizens who have bought into the deception that earth will be invaded by aliens and will pick up their weapons and mobilize to fight against this coming invasion, thinking they are going to save earth and the civilization of mankind.

Therefore, I am cautioning all Christians, pastors, ministers, leaders and all those who love God and his Son, Jesus Christ to not get caught up in Satan's deception by finding yourselves warring against God. As the scriptures say, "Come out from among them, for friendship with the world is enmity with God."

You have been warned!

www.ingramcontent.com/pod-product-compliance
Lightning Source LLC
Chambersburg PA
CBHW030113100526
44591CB00009B/394